# Psalms 1-72

A

*Simple Not Shallow*

*Presentation*

*Translated and edited by*

Charles Yerkes

**Simple Not Shallow Books**
Franklin, Tn

Copyright © 2021 by Charles Yerkes.
All rights reserved.
No part of this publication may be reproduced, stored in a retrieval system or transmitted in any way by any means, electronic, mechanical, photocopy, recording, or otherwise without the prior written permission of Charles Yerkes except as provided by USA copyright law.

Translated and edited by Charles Yerkes

Published by  Simple Not Shallow Books
Email: charles@simplenotshallow.com
Website: www.simplenotshallow.com
Franklin, Tennessee

Book design copyright © 2021 by Charles Yerkes.
Cover and interior design by Charles Yerkes.

ISBN: 9780999636824

Printed in United States of America

Library of Congress Control Number: 2021918946

# Dedication

This is dedicated to all who want
a faith that is growing and vital.
To those who want the abundance of
life that Jesus came to give.

# Contents

Introduction ................................................................................. i

Book 1 (Psalms 1-41) .................................................................. 1

Book 2 (Psalms 42-72) ............................................................ 179

References List: ..................................................................... 330

# Introduction

I want to take a moment and share why this presentation of the Psalms came into being. The short answer is that I have found so many exciting and faith building things in the Psalms, that I simply have to share them. The excitement is too much for me to want to contain it.

I've always enjoyed the Psalms; the imagery, the emotions, and the honesty in communicating with God. Then, once I learned how to read ancient Hebrew, I went back and began reading these wonderful poems in the Hebrew. This is where the excitement really began to build; for I began to see nuances I had always missed out on before.

These I found by spending time with the Hebrew. Spending time with the words and searching out the meanings of the ones I did not know. I also spent time learning, not only the definitions but also how the words were sometimes used. For the two do not always offer the same meaning. We are familiar with this in our own use of English. I'll use the word crushed in two different sentences and you will see what I mean. First, "I crushed an empty soda can." Second, "I crushed that presentation!" In the first, I know you can see that aluminum can being crushed flat. In the second, you understand that I did not flatten the presentation. Rather, that it was extremely well delivered. Languages can be so fun!

As a result of this type of fun, the Psalms started to come alive for me as never before. I began to see more nuance, more shades of texture, and gleaned deeper understandings of the messages contained in the Psalms. It has been a thrilling experience to discover more of the nuances than I could see or appreciate before reading the Hebrew. Nuances which our wonderful translations have difficulty conveying. Do not misunderstand, they do a most excellent job of conveying the meaning; which is the most important part. All nuances can do are to make that meaning more palpable; to help us gain a fuller appreciation of the meaning. It does not create the meaning.

I do want to make this very clear. This presentation of the Psalms is all about added nuance. It is never about a new meaning. God put all the meaning he wanted into the Bible as he inspired the original authors to first write it down, the Psalms included. This meaning has been wonderfully revealed by him for many, many years. He certainly does not need my help in doing so at this time. Indeed, I can boldly say that I have been very purposeful in not adding anything to or taking anything away from the meanings found in the Psalms.

If you are looking for a completely new or novel meaning.... I'm not even sorry for disappointing you. If, instead, you want a richer encounter with the meaning already there, then I hope this will serve you well. For, I am offering a more fleshed out presentation of what is already there. Let me briefly address what this means and what this looks like.

In making the presentation, I used six different lexicons, several scholarly commentaries, and always at least ten accepted Bible translations (see the reference list at the end of this book). This to understand what the verse is saying and to check and triple check my understanding of each one. In doing so, if I found two or more accepted definitions for a word or phrase, and these complemented each other, meaning that they provided a deeper understanding of what is said, I used both.

For example, in Psalm 37:17, I used both definitions for the Hebrew word: זרועות . The direct translation is "arms" and yet here it is used to mean "strength." So, I use both of the definitions found; as follows:

> For the arms,
> The strength,
> Of wickedness
> Will be shattered.

This allowed me to remain true to what is written and to help a modern mindset understand more clearly what is being said.

At other times, if the word or phrase is used elsewhere in Scripture and if the lexicons indicate that this usage may be included in the meaning of its use in the psalm, I incorporated that as well. For example, in Psalm 48:2, the phrase: יַרְכְּתֵי צָפוֹן literally means "far north." But in Isaiah 14:13, it is used in a way that seems to describe Heaven. So, I incorporated both Heaven and the far north in this presentation; which fits rather nicely in the line of adulations for Zion found in Psalm 48. As follows:

> Beautiful and towering,
> A source of joy
> To all the earth,
> Is Mount Zion,
> Heaven,
> The farthest of the north lands.
> The city of the great king.

At other times, I have added a word or phrase that tends to help in understanding the psalm better and still not change the meaning. For example, in Psalm 72, which begins by asking God to give to the king his judgment and his justness. In light of the covenant requirements for keeping God's law being the basis for blessing, I have, at points, inserted the word "Then" to show this relationship, That as long as the king is operating with God's judgment and justness then what is listed afterwards will happen; as in the following three examples:

1)
> Then he will administer
> The help of judgment
> To your people;
> Through your just loyalty.

2)
> Then
> The mountains and the hills
> Will yield peace and deliverance
> To the people,
> Through justice.

3)
> Then
> He will provide
> The poor and needy of the people
> With justice.

And so on. The word "then" does not actually occur, but it seems a proper to use it in these instances. The language does allow for it and this indicates that the king must have God's judgment and justness for any of the blessings to happen. I find this does not change the meaning that the king needs God's help or the desire for blessing. It also highlights the nuance of something David would have been vitally aware of, God's covenant with himself and with Israel. For the keeping of God's law and the use of God's judgment and justness were absolutely necessary; if the blessings were to follow.

    Finally, you will notice the arrangement of the words on the page. Here I took some scholarly poetic license and arranged the words in a more poetic fashion. One meant to give emphasis to words and ideas. As well as help the eye flow more smoothly over the Psalms. At least, that is the intent.

I do hope that you find this presentation to be refreshing and exciting as you read the nuances found. If you have any questions concerning how a particular phrase is presented; feel free to ask. Contact me through my website: www.simplenotshallow.com. I'm always more than happy to hold honest conversations concerning this.

As to the reason why I only have the first 72 Psalms in this book. The Psalms are officially grouped into five books. The second book ends with Psalm 72. As that is about halfway through the Psalms, it makes a convenient place to end this first book. The rest will follow when I have finished the work on all 150 psalms.

My prayer is that you will find this to be a wonderful resource for growing closer to God. That you find it helpful and that you find as much excitement in it as I have found. That it will be a useful tool in helping you grow in your relationship with God.

Charles Yerkes

# Book 1
## Psalms 1-41

# Psalm 1

¹To be happy,
A man will not walk according
To the advice of the wicked,
Advice that considers not God.
He will not travel down the path belonging
To those who have strayed and missed the mark.
Nor will he keep company with
Those who are the scoffers,
The chronic and unthinking skeptics.

²And, if the instruction of our Lord
Is his delight
And on his instructions
He will muse day and night,
He will be happy.
He will be
³As a tree transplanted by channels of water.
Whose fruit
It will yield in its season
And whose leaf
Will neither wither nor waste away.
He will succeed in all that he does.

⁴Not so the wicked.
Rather, they are like the useless chaff,
Which is scattered and driven about by the wind.

⁵For this reason, they will not
Be able
To maintain their courage
In the day of judgment;
They will not
Be able
To stand their ground.
Nor will those,
Who have strayed and missed the mark,
Be able
To stand in the company of those
Who have remained true.

⁶For the Lord values and watches
Over the righteous.
But the way of the wicked
Will vanish and become lost.

# Psalm 2

¹Why have the nations been restless?
Why will the people scheme in futility?
²The kings of the earth resist
And the dignitaries conspire together
Against the Lord
And against his anointed.
³Saying,
"We will tear their restraints on us apart;
We will throw off their control."

⁴Sitting in the heavens,
The Lord laughs and is at his ease;
He is not bothered by them.
Though, he is not amused by them either;
For he holds their thoughts in disdain.
⁵And he will speak to them in his anger;
And in burning anger
He will terrify them by saying,
⁶"I have consecrated my king on Zion,
My holy mountain."

⁷Now, I will tell you of
The decree of the Lord.
He said to me,
"You are my son.
Today I have brought you forth.
⁸Ask of me
And I will give you
These nations as an inheritance.
And for your possession,
The very ends of the earth.
⁹You will smash your enemies.
As, with a rod of iron,
You would smash
The clay vessels of a potter."

¹⁰And now, O kings, act prudently.
Allow yourselves to be instructed,
O rulers of the earth.
¹¹Serve the Lord with reverence
And rejoice with trembling.
¹²Pay homage to the son,
Acknowledge him as king.
Otherwise, the Lord will become angry;
Or, if you stray from the way
Of the righteous,
His anger will soon burn.
Happy are they who seek refuge in him.

# Psalm 3

¹My Lord,
How my enemies
Have increased in number.
Many are rising against me.
²Many are saying of me,
"For him,
There is no help from God."

³But you,
My Lord,
Are my protection;
The one whom I glorify,
And the one
Who confers honor upon me.

⁴My voice I will raise to the Lord
And he will answer from is holy mountain.

⁵I lie down, I sleep, and I awaken
Because the Lord gives me
The strength to do so.
⁶So, I will not be afraid of the vast hordes
Of people who surround me
And who pit themselves against me.

⁷Arise,
My Lord.
Rescue me,
My God!
For it is you
Who strikes all of
My enemies on the cheek,
Bringing disgrace upon them.
And it is you
Who smashes the teeth of the wicked,
Making them powerless.

⁸Deliverance and rescue
Come from God.
And my Lord,
Your blessing
Is upon your people.

# Psalm 4

[1]God,
My Sovereign,
When I call for help,
Answer me.
For you are the one
Who dispenses justice to me.
In my previous distress
You freed me from my need.
Be generous to me
Once again and
Hear my prayer.

²Sons of men,
How long will you love
Empty expressions
And seek to hurt with a lie?

³Know this,
My Lord treats those
Who are faithful to him
Extremely well.
My Lord will hear
When I call to him.

⁴So, in awe,
Be excited;
But sin not.
The solitude of your room
Is the place
To scream aloud
As you think things through.
⁵Offer the right sacrifices
And trust in our Lord.

⁶My Lord,
Many are saying,
"Who will show us
Happiness and prosperity?"
Shine your favor upon us that they may see.

⁷For you have placed
Joy in my heart.
More than they have
In a time of great abundance,
In times when they have
Much grain and wine.
And because of this,
⁸In peace, I will
Both lie down and sleep.
Because, you alone,
My Lord,
Are responsible
For the security
In which I dwell.

# Psalm 5

¹My Lord,
Listen favorably to my words;
Pay careful attention to my whispered prayers.
²My King and my God,
Pay special attention to
The sound of my cries for help.
For it is to you and you alone that I pray.

³My Lord,
In the morning you hear my voice.
And in the morning, I make ready
And expectantly watch for you.

⁴For you are not a God who takes delight
In wrongs or offenses given.
Indeed, evil cannot reside in your presence;
It cannot be a guest in your house.
⁵Those infatuated with themselves
Are not able
To make their stand or hold their ground
Before you.
You hate all who practice injustice.
⁶You judge and destroy the liars.
You, my Lord,
Regard men of blood and treachery
As abominations.

⁷But as for me,
In the greatness of your abundant kindness,
I will enter into your house.
At the temple of your holiness
I will submit to you in devotion.
⁸My Lord,
Lead me in your justness.
On account of my enemies,
On account of those
Who treacherously watch everything,
Make your way level and even before me.

⁹For in their mouths there are no true words.
Who they are... is an all-consuming ruin.
Their throats are open graves;
For with their tongues, they flatter.

¹⁰Sovereign God,
Declare them guilty and make them pay.
Let them fall as a result of their own plans.
Because of their many crimes and transgressions
Scatter them and isolate them from one another.
For they are recalcitrant against you.

¹¹But all who take refuge in you
Will rejoice forever.
They will repeatedly
Shout for joy.
You will surround them
With your protection,
Causing them to be
Inaccessible to those
Who would do them harm.
Even so,
Those who love your name
Will rejoice in you.
¹²For you,
My Lord,
Continually bless the righteous.
You surround them with favor,
As with a large shield.

# Psalm 6

¹My Lord,
Do not punish me while you are angry.
And do not discipline me while your anger burns.
²Show mercy to me, my Lord,
For I am fragile.
Heal me, for I am so horror struck
That I feel it in my bones.
³My soul is greatly dismayed.
But you,
My Lord,
Until when... how long?

⁴Return my Lord
And rescue my soul.
Liberate me,
On account of your loving kindness.
⁵For the dead cannot speak of you.
For who can praise you from the grave?

⁶I have grown weary from crying out.
Every night I cause my bed
To swim in the flood of my tears.
⁷My eyes swell and darken
From worry;
They have grown old
Because of all my adversaries.

⁸Turn away from me,
All you who practice evil,
For the Lord has heard
The sound of my weeping.
⁹The Lord has heard
My plea for mercy.
The Lord has found
My prayer acceptable.

¹⁰All of my enemies will be disgraced
And so greatly dismayed
That they won't know what to do.
They will turn away from me,
And in that moment
They will feel their shame.

# Psalm 7

¹My Lord,
My God,
It is in you
That I take refuge.
So, save me from
All who persecute me.
Deliver me!
²Lest they tear my soul
As a lion would;
Tearing me to pieces
While no one rescues me.

³My Lord,
My God,
If I have done this thing,
If there is injustice in what I do,
⁴If I do evil to my friend,
Or without cause,
Pillage an enemy.
⁵Then allow my enemy to
Pursue me and collect my soul.
Allow him to trample my life
Into the ground
And to lay my honor
In the dust of humiliation and death.

⁶Arise my Lord.
In your anger assert yourself
Against the rage of my attackers.
Arouse yourself on my behalf;
According to the decision,
The judgment,
That you have commanded.
⁷And gather an assembly of nations around you
And return your judgment upon them from on high.

⁸The Lord will execute judgment upon the nations,
Calling them to account for themselves.
Exonerate me, my Lord,
On account of that
Which is in me,
Both righteousness and purity.
⁹Avenge the evil done by the wicked;
Bring it to an end.
But firmly establish the righteous.
As you,
O righteous God,
Put to the test their moral character
And their deepest secrets.

¹⁰Sovereign God
Has undertaken my defense.
He is the one who helps
The righteous heart.
¹¹Sovereign God
Is a righteous judge
And he is a God who
Shows his righteous anger
Every day.
¹²If a man will not turn
And keep his whole life
Turned towards God,
God will sharpen his sword.
He will bend and string his bow.
Making them both ready for war.
¹³He will prepare his weapons of death;
He will make his arrows into shafts of fire.

¹⁴Listen well;
He who is pregnant with imminent disaster,
Who conceives harm and who gives birth
To that which deceives and betrays,
¹⁵This man has dug a pit and dug it deep.
But it is he who will fall into the trap
Which he has made.
¹⁶The harm he intends will be returned upon him.
The violence he intends will descend,
Landing upon his own head.

¹⁷I will give thanks and praise to the Lord,
On account of his righteousness.
I will praise the name of
The Lord Most High.

# Psalm 8

¹Lord,
Our God and Sovereign,
How magnificent is your name
In all the earth.
You,
Who have displayed your majesty in the heavens.
²You,
Who have destined your defenses to be made
Through the mouths of children and nursing babes;
For the sake of your enemies.
In order to remove those who are hostile
And,
Those who are vindictive to you.

³As I gaze upon your heavens,
The work of your fingers,
The moon and the stars,
Which you have set in place.

⁴What are human beings
That you will remember them?
Or the individual
That you will pay special attention to him?

⁵And yet,
You have deprived him of little,
In comparison to the heavenly beings.
You have crowned him with honor and splendor.
⁶You have made him a lord over all you have made.
You have placed all things under his authority,
⁷All sheep, cattle, and wild animals too.
⁸The birds of the air,
The fish of the sea,
And everything which passes through the sea.

⁹Lord,
Our God and Sovereign,
How magnificent is your name in all the earth.

# Psalm 9

¹I will worship and praise
Sovereign God,
With my whole heart.
I will tell of all the miraculous things
Which you have done.
²I will merrily rejoice and revel
In you.
I will praise your name,
The name above all names.

³When my enemies
Were repelled,
They stumbled backwards,
All over themselves,
And were carried off before you.
⁴For you
Have executed judgment
In favor of me and my legal claim.
From the judge's seat,
You
Have presided and passed
A virtuous judgment.
⁵You
Have rebuked the people.
You
Have destroyed the wicked.
You
Have eradicated their names...
Forever.

⁶The enemy has vanished,
Ruined forever.
Their cities you have torn down.
They, the very memory of them,
Has been lost.

⁷The Lord will reign forever.
He has established
His throne
As a seat of judgment.
⁸He will judge
The inhabitants of the world.
Because he is loyal to them,
He executes judgment
Towards the people in fairness.
⁹And the Lord is also
A haven for the oppressed,
A shelter in times of need.

¹⁰Those who know your name
Will trust you.
For you,
My Lord,
Do not abandon
Those who seek you
In prayer and praise.

¹¹Sing
To the Lord who dwells in Zion;
Proclaim
His deeds to the nations.

¹²For he,
Who requires a life
For bloodshed,
Remembers the oppressed.
He
Does not forget
The calls for help
Made by the dejected,
In their times of need.

¹³Be gracious to me,
My Lord.
Look after my misery;
Misery caused
By those who hate me.
Elevate me
From the gates of death.
¹⁴So that,
In the gates of the daughter of Zion,
In the gates of Jerusalem,
I may proclaim
All the praise that belongs to you.
I will shout in celebration of
Your help,
Of the deliverance
You
Have provided.

¹⁵The people have fallen
Into the trap which they have made.
Their own foot
Is trapped in the net that they
Had secretly laid out for others.
¹⁶The Lord
Has revealed himself.
He has made his judgment;
The wicked
Have ensnared themselves
By their own actions.
¹⁷The wicked,
All the people who forget God,
Will turn towards the home of the dead.

[18] For the needy
Will not always be forgotten.
Nor will the hope
Of the poor, the destitute,
Be lost forever.

[19] Arise my Lord!
Do not let men defy you.
Let the people be judged by you.
[20] Put terror into them,
My Lord.
Let them know
They are
But men;
They are
But mere human beings.

# Psalm 10

¹My Lord,
Why do you stay so distant?
Why do you shut your eyes to times of need?

²In arrogance,
The wicked individual
Aggressively pursues those in need....

Let him be trapped
In the schemes
Which he has planned for the needy.

³For the wicked one rejoices
In the cravings of his soul
And he breaks away.
Blessing himself
While discarding the Lord.

⁴In his pretentiousness,
The wicked one thinks an accounting
Is not required.
In all his scheming,
There is no God;
His ways will be successful.

⁵At all times,
My Lord,
Your high decisions, judgments, and laws
Are far from him.
He scoffs at all his enemies.
⁶He says to himself,
"I am secure; I will not falter.
I am protected from misfortune."

⁷His mouth is full
Of cursing, fraud, and oppression.
Under his tongue lies the source
Of another's need
And impending disaster.

⁸He sits in ambush,
Near the villages.
And from his secret hiding place
He ruthlessly
Kills the blameless.
His eyes always search
For the unhappy helpless.

⁹He lies in ambush,
In his hiding place,
As a lion crouched
And hidden in a thicket.
He lies in ambush
To catch the needy.
And he catches them
As he pulls them
Into his net.

¹⁰The disheartened are crushed
By his mighty strengths.
They cower and they fall.
¹¹The wicked one says to himself,
"God has forgotten them.
He hides his face.
He will not see what I do, ever."

¹²Arise my Lord,
My God.
Raise your hand to strike back,
To...
Do something.
Do not forget those who are
Humbly bowed before you.

¹³On what basis
Does the wicked one
Discard God?
On what basis
Has he convinced himself
That you
Will not require
An accounting for
What he has done?

¹⁴For you do see
The harm and the vexation.
You do look upon these
In order to take them into your hand;
To become involved
And require that accounting.
The helpless...
Leave it in your hands;
They entrust it into your keeping.
For you have been the one
Who assists the fatherless,
The ones who
Cannot help themselves.

¹⁵Shatter the strength of evil
And of the evil one.
Require an accounting of his offenses.
Do not allow him to escape this.

¹⁶The Lord is king;
He reigns forever and ever.
Wicked people are
Carried off from his land.

¹⁷My Lord,
You have heard
The longings of those
Humbly bowed before you.
You are intent upon their hearts.
You cause your ear to attend to them.
¹⁸You vindicate
The fatherless and the oppressed.
The people of your land
Will never be terrified again.

# Psalm 11

¹I take refuge in the Lord.
So, how will you say to me,
"Hastily, like a bird, fly away.
²For behold, the wicked
Have bent the bow.
They have notched the arrow
And taken aim.
This, in order to shoot
From the darkness
At the upright in heart.
³The foundations of our society
Are in ruins.
So,
What can the righteous achieve?"

⁴Our Lord is in his temple.
Our Lord's throne is in heaven.
His eyes will see everything.
And a flashing glance
From his eyes
Will put the sons of men to the test;
It will search them through and through.

⁵Our Lord will put to the test
Both the righteous and the wicked.

And his very soul hates
The loving of violence and ruthlessness.
⁶His judgment will fall upon the wicked,
Like burning coals
Of fire and brimstone
Raining down upon them.
And a scorching whirlwind
Will be their allotment.

⁷For our Lord is righteous
And he loves
Loyalty, honesty, and righteous conduct.
It is the honest,
It is the just,
And it is the upright
Who will enter his presence,
Who will see his face, and
Who will experience his favor.

# Psalm 12

[1]My Lord,
Help us!
For faithfulness has
Come to an end.
The godly,
Are no more.
The trustworthy have
Disappeared
From the race of man.
[2]Companions now speak empty and
Unrestrained words to each other.
They speak with a smooth tongue,
Flattering lips, and
A double dealing heart.

³Now, our Lord
Will completely destroy
All flattering lips and
The tongues that speak in arrogance.
⁴The ones that have said,
"Because of our tongues, we are strong.
Our flattering lips help us.
Who is greater that we are?"

⁵But our Lord has said,
"Because of the oppression of those in need,
Because of their groans of distress,
I will now arise and
Come to their aid.
I will bring security to those in need,
To the ones against whom
These flatterers rage."

⁶Our Lord's words are purely spoken.
They are honorable and
Full of integrity.
They are as pure as silver
That has been refined
In the fires of the crucible.
Indeed, as pure as silver
Refined seven times;
Nothing is purer than this.

⁷My Lord,
You will take care of those in need.
You will watch over us;
From this evil generation to...
Forever.

⁸For the wicked will roam everywhere,
When thoughtlessness
Is exalted among the people.

# Psalm 13

¹How long,
My Lord,
Will I be forgotten by you?
Forever?
How long
Will you hide your face from me?
How long
Will you withhold your favor?
²How long
Must anxiety grip my soul?
Must agony grip my heart every day?
How long
Will my enemy proudly overshadow me?

³Look at me and give me an answer,
My Lord,
My God.
Fill my eyes with your light,
Otherwise, I will be
As the sleeping dead.
⁴And my enemy will say,
"I have prevailed over him."
And my foes will rejoice
Because I have been
Undone and overthrown.

⁵But I have trusted
In your loving kindness.
My heart will shout
While rejoicing in your assistance.
⁶I will sing in praise
Of you, my Lord.
Because of what you have done for me.

# Psalm 14

¹It is the fool,
The irreligious unbeliever,
Who has said in his heart,
"There is no God."
These have perverted themselves
And are corrupt.
Their deeds are done in a loathsome
And heinous manner.
There is none truly doing good.

²Our Lord, from heaven,
Has looked down
Upon all of mankind.
To see whether there are any
Who have insight and act prudently;
For any who search intently for him.

³But, as one, they have all fallen;
They have all revolted and
Turned from the right path.
They have turned from God.
They are morally corrupt,
Tainted, and confused.
No, there is none
Truly doing good.
There is not even one.

⁴Have they not,
All those who cause sorrow
By doing evil,
Have they not
Learned their bitter lesson?
All those who devour my people,
Who make a meal out of them;
The same as they do with bread.
All those who do not call upon the Lord.

⁵They will find no satisfaction in this meal.
For then, they will quake and tremble with dread
Because God abides with all who are righteous.

⁶You act shamefully in your plans
Directed against the poor;
Because the Lord is their refuge.

⁷Oh, that God's help for Israel
Would come from Zion now.
For when the Lord
Restores the fortunes of his people,
Jacob will shout in triumph and
Israel will rejoice.

# Psalm 15

¹My Lord,
Who is the one,
Foreign to your land,
Who may yet reside
In your hospitality,
In your sanctuary?
Who may settle down
On your holy mountain?

²The one who walks
In honesty,
Who does what is right, and
Who speaks the truth from his heart.

³The one who does not
Slander with his tongue,
Who does no wrong to a friend, and
Who brings no reproach upon his family.

⁴The one who views
The reprobate as despicable
But who honors those who honor God.

The one who stands
By his oath, even when
It is to his disadvantage to do so;
He is disadvantaged, and he does not change.

⁵The one who does not lend
His money at interest and
Who does not accept
A bribe against the blameless.

The one who does these things,
He is forever secure;
He will not stumble on his way.

# Psalm 16

¹Take care of me,
My God.
For it is in you alone
That I seek protection.

²I have said to God,
"You are my Lord.
My happiness and well-being are
Not valued more highly than you are.
For I have no good apart from you."

³To the holy ones who are in the land,
They are the majestic ones and
All my delight is in them.
⁴To them I say,
"Those who have acquired another god,
Their hurt and pain will greatly increase.
Such is the dowry they will pay."

I will not devote a drink offering
To their libations of blood.
I will not make an offering
To their gods.
Nor will I even speak their names.

⁵For you,
My Lord,
Are my inheritance, my portion,
And my cup of fate and blessing.
You hold my destiny in your hands.
⁶The boundary lines allotted to me
Are in delightful places;
My inheritance contains rich soil indeed.
Yes, I am pleased
With this beautiful inheritance.

⁷I praise my Lord,
Who advises me.
Indeed, in the hours of darkness
My heart and mind discipline me.
⁸For I have placed my attention
Continuously upon my Lord.
And because he is at my right hand,
I will not be shaken.

⁹Because of this,
My heart is merry.
And all that is noble within me
Rejoices.
And my body settles down
And dwells in security.

¹⁰For you will not leave
My soul in the abode of the dead.
Nor will you surrender
Your faithful ones to the grave.

¹¹Declare and make known to me
The way
That leads to life.
For it is in your presence
That the fullness of all joy is found.
Happiness is at your right hand...
Forever.

# Psalm 17

[1]My Lord,
Hear justness;
Hear what is right.
Listen attentively
To my prayerful cries of lament.
Heed my prayer.
Made in words that contain
No fraud, trickery, nor deal making.
My honest prayer to you.

[2]Let the judgment of me
Come from you.
Let your eyes see
The honesty and the integrity.

³You have examined my heart.
In the hours of darkness,
You have made a careful inspection of it.
In order to hold me accountable.
You have refined my heart
Through fire,
Burning out the impurity.
You will find that I have
Not planned to do evil.
Nor does evil
Pour out of my mouth.

⁴In terms of how a man acts,
By following the instruction of your words,
I have been watchful and observant.
In order to avoid
The ways of the violent,
The ways of the thief.
⁵I have firmly kept my foot steps
In the tracks you have made.
And my steps have not faltered.

⁶I have called out to you,
My God;
Because you will respond to me.
Please, turn your attention unto me and
Hear what I am saying.
⁷Show me your marvelous concern,
Oh, helper of those
Seeking refuge in your strength.
Refuge from those rising against them.
⁸Please protect me
As one does the pupil,
The daughter of the eye.
In the protection of your wings,
⁹Shelter me from the wicked
Who
Deal violently with me.
Shelter me from my mortal enemies
Who surround me.

¹⁰They have shut
All warmth out of their hearts.
And with their mouths,
They are coldly presumptuous.
¹¹They have tracked me down
And now surround me.
Their eyes are set,
Fixed in their desire
To stretch me out
On the ground.
¹²Like a lion burning with desire
To tear apart its prey;
Like a hungry young lion
Ready to pounce
From its hiding place.

¹³Arise,
My Lord.
Confront these lions and bring them down.
Deliver me from these wicked ones.
With your sword, save me.
¹⁴My Lord,
With the strength of your hand
Deliver me from these God-less ones,
From the peoples of this world.
From those
Whose chosen inheritance is in this life.
Whose appetites are satisfied
With merely the good things you provide.
With merely taking satisfaction in
Having many children;
With merely bequeathing their abundance
To their children.

¹⁵But as for me,
In righteousness I will behold your face.
My appetites will only be satisfied
When I am awakened in your presence.

# Psalm 18

[1] I love you,
My Lord,
My strength.
My Lord,
You are
[2] My mountain fortress
And my deliverer.
My God,
My mountain,
The one in whom I take refuge.
My protector,
The source and strength of my salvation,
You are
My stronghold.

³My Lord,
The one worthy of praise,
To you, I called out for help.
And I received help.
I was liberated
From those, hostile to me.
⁴For I was surrounded
By the entrapments of death;
Torrents of worthlessness...
Trenches of death...
These terrified me.

⁵The nets of the underworld
Surrounded me;
The snares of death
Had come to greet me.
⁶And in my distress,
I shouted to you
My Lord.
It was to you,
My God,
That I cried out for help.
And you heard my voice.
In your heavenly abode,
You heard me.
You heard my screams for help.

⁷ And what you heard made you angry.
And in response,
The earth rose and fell loudly;
It quaked as never before.
The very foundations of the mountains
Trembled.
Moving ceaselessly,
Restlessly
As they too loudly rose and fell.
⁸Smoke
Came from your nose
And fire
From your mouth;
Burning coals
That consumed whatever they touched.
⁹And the sky bowed low
As you descended.
There were darkened storm clouds
Under your feet.
¹⁰And you drove upon a cherub,
Your living chariot,
And you flew.
You swooped down on the wings of the wind.

¹¹You made the darkness to be your cover;
Surrounding yourself with
Masses of tumultuous storm clouds.
¹²Before you,
And out of the flashing brightness
That lanced through that darkness,
Came hailstones and coals of fire;
Coming and passing through your clouds.
¹³You,
My Lord,
Caused the sky to thunder
As you,
The Most High,
Raised your voice,
The hailstones and coals of fire.
¹⁴You let loose with your arrows
And scattered my enemies.
With great flashes of lightening
You caused them
To scurry away in confusion.
¹⁵My Lord,
At your expression of disapproval,
At the merest breath of your wrath,
Even the deepest valley in the sea
Becomes visible and uncovered.
The very foundation of the created world
Becomes exposed.

ⁱ⁶ And you reached down from heaven
And caught hold of me.
You pulled me out of those deep waters.
¹⁷ You snatched me away
From my formidable and fierce enemy
And from those who hated me;
Because they were too strong for me.
¹⁸ When they accosted me
It was my day of final disaster.
But you,
My Lord,
Were my support.
¹⁹ You freed me from their grasp.
You rescued me
Because you are delighted and
Pleased with me.

[20] My Lord,
You have treated me according to my loyalty,
According to the cleanliness of my hands,
My unstained loyalty to you.
And you
Have returned loyalty to me.
[21] For I have stuck to the agreements,
To the conduct that my Lord requires.
And I am not guilty
Of turning away from my God.
[22] For all your decisions, your judgments,
Are present with me.
I have not pushed aside
Your laws or your decrees.
[23] With you,
I have been full of integrity
And I have kept myself from misdeeds,
From the sin
To which I would otherwise be prone.
[24] And you,
My Lord,
Have paid me back in kind.
You have given...
A very appropriate return for my loyalty.
For you do see that my hands are indeed clean.

²⁵ With the faithful,
You prove yourself faithful.
With the strong, and the blameless,
You prove blameless.
²⁶ And to the honest man,
You prove honest.
Yet, to those who are violent,
You will act violently.
And with the twisted and the false,
You prove full of twists and turns.
²⁷ For you help the humble,
But the arrogant, you humiliate.
²⁸ My Lord,
You have caused my lamp to shine forth.
My God,
You shine your light upon my distress;
You illuminate my darkness.
²⁹ Because of you,
I was able to break through these barriers.
Because of you,
My God,
I was able to escape over that wall.

³⁰God,
Your ways, your methods are sound.
They are full of integrity and perfect.
The words of my Lord
Have passed through my fiery ordeals
And have proven true.
He is the protection
Of all who take refuge with him.
³¹For who is God
Besides our Lord?
And who is a rock, a place of safe refuge,
Except our God?
³²The God,
Who surrounds me with strength
And makes my way, my conduct,
To be impeccable,
Full of integrity, and without reproach.
³³You make my feet
To be like those of a deer;
You set me, sure footed,
Upon the mountain ridge.
³⁴You teach my hands how to fight.
And you train my arms to be strong;
So, they may pull back on a bow of bronze.
³⁵You have given me
The protection of your deliverance
And your right hand
Supports and sustains me.
And your humility, meekness, and gentleness
Make me great.
³⁶You have given me
A broad flat space with firm footing
On which to step.
And my feet have not stumbled.

³⁷I did pursue and catch my enemies.
And I did not turn away until
I had put an end to their hostilities.
³⁸I have smashed their ability to harm me
And they are no longer able to rise against me.
For they have fallen under my feet.
³⁹For you surrounded me
With the strength for the battle.
And you have caused
Those who stood against me
To bow down before me.
⁴⁰You have made those of hostile intent
To flee from me;
And those who hated me
To be ruined.
⁴¹They screamed out for help,
But there were no great heroes to save them.
They even cried out to you,
My Lord.
But you refused to answer them.
⁴²My enemies have been crushed,
Scattered,
Like so much dust in the wind.
Like the mire in the streets,
They have been thrown out.

⁴³You
Saved me from the hostilities of those people.
You
Have installed me as the leader of nations.
Peoples I had never heard of
Now serve me, are now my subjects.
Even when all they hear about me is hearsay,
Yet still they hear me;
They listen and obey.
⁴⁴These foreign sons cringe and fawn on me
As they feign obedience.
⁴⁵They do so because
They are now discouraged and have lost heart.
And so, they come trembling with fear
From out of their prison,
The prison that is their stronghold.
⁴⁶For my Lord is alive and well.
Blessed and full of strength is
My rock,
My safe refuge.
And the God
Of my deliverance
Will be exalted.
⁴⁷My God,
The one who avenges me
As he puts to flight and subdues these nations.
Causing them to bow to my authority.
⁴⁸The one who saves me from those of hostile intent.
Yes!
You
Exalt me, by
Standing me above my enemies.
You have rescued me from the violent.

⁴⁹My Lord,
Therefore, I will praise you
Among the nations.
Of your name
Will I sing.
⁵⁰Magnifying your rescue
Of the one you made king.
And how you
Are kind and good
To the one you anointed,
To David and
To his descendants, forever.

# Psalm 19

¹The heavens make known the splendor and
The high honor that belongs to God.
The sky confronts us with the work of his hands.

²Day to day, this news goes forth.
Night to night, this knowledge is declared.

³There is no speech,
There are no words,
Their voice is not heard.
⁴Yet, in all the world,
Their message is heard.
And their words,
To the very ends of the earth.

For it is in them
That he established a home for the sun.
⁵Which, is like one newly married
Striding forth from the bridal chamber.
And like a valiant messenger
Who rejoices in running on his way.
⁶From the edge of one horizon, it departs
And runs its circuitous course to the other,
Where the day turns into night.
And there is nothing hidden
From the glow of the sun;
By it, everything is seen.

⁷So too, are the words of my Lord.

The instructions of my Lord are perfect.
They are wholesome and full of integrity,
Restoring liveliness to the soul.
The statements of my Lord
Are trustworthy for making the naïve wise.
⁸The procedures of my Lord
Are just, making the heart merry.
The commandment of my Lord is pure;
It gives light and sparkle to the eyes.
⁹The fear of my Lord, these revered laws...
His religion,
Is pure in ethic and endures forever.
The judgments of my Lord are truth
And they are all together just.
¹⁰They are more desirable than gold,
Than much fine gold.
And they are sweeter than honey,
Than pure honey straight off the comb.
What's more,
¹¹By them your servant is made alert.
By them your servant can hear and heed a warning.
In observing them,
In living them out,
There is much that is gained.

¹²Who can consider or even perceive transgressions
Made through ignorance?
Please, pardon me for those transgressions,
The ones hidden from my awareness;
Those my ignorance has kept secret from me.
And more than this,
¹³Keep me, your servant, back
From those that are known;
Those chosen in a moment of insolence.
Keep me humble,
That they may not control me.
For then I will be complete,
I will be whole.
And I will be blameless
Of great apostasy,
Of greatly turning my back towards you.
¹⁴Let my words and the musings of my heart
Be those which find favor with you,
My Lord,
My rock.
The one who redeems me.

# Psalm 20

¹May the Lord answer you in the day of distress.
And the name of the God of Jacob,
His power and his splendor,
Protect you.
²May he send you help from the holy sanctuary
And from Zion sustain you.
³May he remember all your offerings
And accept your burnt sacrifice;
May he remember your devotions
And grant you, his favor.
⁴May he give to you according to your heart
And carry out all your plans.
⁵May we rejoice over God helping you.
And in the name of our God,
May we unfurl our flag.
May the Lord fulfill all your desires.

⁶Now I know that our Lord
Will deliver his anointed one.
From his holy heaven,
He will answer him with a mighty miracle.
By the might of his own hand,
Our Lord will deliver him.

⁷These will sing the praise of their chariots.
Those... their horses.
But we sing the praise
Of the name of the Lord our God.
⁸They buckle at the knee and fall into ruin.
But we arise, stand together, and are restored.

⁹Our Lord will save the king.
He will answer when we call.

# Psalm 21

[1]Our Lord,
In your protection the king will rejoice.
And of your help,
of your victories,
He will greatly shout in jubilation.
[2]For you have given him
The desire of his heart.
And you have not refused
The desires that his lips
Have made known.
[3]For you meet him with
Blessings of good things.
And you place on is head
A crown of pure gold.

⁴He asked from you, life.
And you gave to him a length of days...
Lasting forever.
⁵With you help his reputation is great;
You have placed upon him
Both majesty and dignity.
⁶Because
You have appointed him,
To forever be
A source of blessing.
And you have made him joyful
With the mirth of your presence.

⁷For the king trusts in the Lord.
And by the gracious faithfulness
Of the Most High,
He will stand firm;
He will not falter.

⁸Our Lord,
May your hand come and light
Upon all your enemies.
Your right hand
Upon those who hate you.
⁹For, when you arrive,
Your presence
Will make them as if
They were in a fiery furnace.
The Lord's anger will engulf them
And the fire will consume them.
¹⁰You will cause their fruit, their influence,
To vanish from the earth.
And their seed, their legacy,
From among the sons of men.
¹¹For they have aggressively turned evil
And against you.
They have schemed a wicked plan.
But they will not prevail,
They will achieve nothing.
¹²For you will oblige them to tuck tail and run,
When your bow strings are bent
And your drawn arrows are facing them.

¹³Rise up, our Lord, in your might.
And we...
We will sing about and praise your strength.

# Psalm 22

¹My God...
My God...
Why have you abandoned me?
Why are your saving acts
So far removed from my screams for help?

²My God,
I call by day
But you do not answer;
By night I am not silent
But I can find no rest.

³Yet, you are holy.
You are firmly seated
In Israel's songs of praise.
⁴In you, our fathers trusted;
They trusted
And you delivered them.
⁵They cried out to you for help
And they were led to safety.
They trusted in you
And were not put to shame;
They were not disappointed in you.

⁶But I...
I am a worm and not a man.
An object of reproach to men
And am despicable to the people.
⁷All who see me ridicule me.
They open their mouths wide to mock me;
As they wag their heads while saying,
⁸"Roll all your distress onto God.
Let his Lord bring him relief.
Let his Lord pull him into safety.
For his Lord takes such delight in him."

⁹Yet,
You are the one
Who pulled me out of the womb.
You are the one
Who inspired confidence in me;
From the very beginning,
Even as my mother nursed me.
¹⁰I came out of the womb
Depending upon you.
From my birth
You have been my God.
¹¹Do not abandon me.
Do not keep your distance,
For my need is near.
For there is no other who can help.

¹²Many are the bullish enemies
That surround me.
Powerful enemies,
Like the fierce bulls of Bashan.
They are full of strength and anger
And they surround me, expectantly.
¹³They open their mouths wide against me,
Like a roaring lion
Set to tear apart its prey.

¹⁴Like water that has been poured out,
So is my strength gone from me.
All my bones are dislocated.
My heart is like wax,
It has melted within me.
¹⁵My strength is dried up,
As dry as a broken piece of pottery.
I cannot even defend myself with words
As my tongue clings to the roof of my mouth.
And you have brought me down
To the world of the dead.

¹⁶For dogs now surround me.
A pack of evil dogs has encircled me,
And are closing in.
Like a lion
They tear at my hands and my feet.
¹⁷I am so wasted away
That I can count
Each and every one of my bones.
And they look on
With immense satisfaction.
¹⁸They divide up my garments among themselves;
They throw dice for my clothing.

¹⁹But you,
My Lord,
Do not be distant;
Do not abandon me.
My strength,
My help,
Hurry now to help me.
²⁰Snatch my life away from the sword;
Snatch my lonely and deserted life away from
The violence of these dogs.
²¹Save me from the mouth of this lion
And from the horns of these wild bulls!

²²You have answered me.
I will recount your name to my brothers.
In the midst of the worshiping assembly
I will give thanks and praise to you.

²³You who revere our Lord,
Praise Him!
All you children of Jacob,
Honor Him!
All you children of Israel,
Stand in awe before Him!
²⁴For he has not despised nor spurned
The suffering of the one in need.
And he has not turned his attention from him.
And when he called to Him for help,
He heard and answered.

²⁵From with you,
My Lord,
And from what you have done,
Comes my song of praise.
In the great worshiping assembly
My vows I will fulfill,
In front of all those who revere you.

$^{26}$Let those who bow before you,
Those who are the humble,
Let them eat and eat their fill.
Let those who worship and petition the Lord,
Praise Him!
Let that which drives you,
Your heart, your courage, and your joy
Live forever!
$^{27}$Let all the extreme ends of the earth
Remember and return to the Lord!
Let all the people
In every nation
Bow down in reverence before him.
$^{28}$For the Lord is the King.
And he does rule
Over all people
In every nation.

²⁹ All those who have had a life of pleasure,
Who have eaten of the good life,
And have now departed from this earth,
Will bow down in reverence.
And all who have not,
But who have gone down
To the dust of the grave,
Will also kneel before him.
For none can bring themselves back to life.

³⁰ The children... they will honor him.
They will tell about my Lord
To the future generations.
³¹ They will come and declare
To a people not yet born,
How his justice set things right.

# Psalm 23

[1] My Lord shepherds me;
I will lack...
Nothing.
[2] He will allow me to lie down
In grassy
Green pastures.
He will escort me to
Water,
In a place of rest.
[3] My soul,
He will refresh.

He will conduct me
Through the wilderness,
On the firm path
Of well living.
This
For his name's sake,
On account of his character.

⁴And even though
I will walk
Through the valley of
Impenetrable gloom, extreme danger,
And even of death;
I will not fear misfortune.
For you,
My Lord,
Will be with me.
Your protective club and
Supportive staff,
Will encourage me.

⁵Before me,
To the mortification of those
Hostile to me,
You will set in order
A ceremonial table at which
To worship you.
You will refresh my head with oil
At the meal of thanksgiving.
There will be more blessings
Than my cup
Can contain.

⁶Indeed,
This prosperity and kindness
Will pursue me
All the days of my life.
And I will return to
The house of my Lord,
For as long as I am alive.

# Psalm 24

¹The earth belongs to the Lord,
And that which fills it;
All the land fit for habitation
And those who inhabit it.
²For he has placed its foundation
Against the chaos of the seas;
Against the chaos found in the sea currents
He has established it.

³Who will go up
Upon the mountain of the Lord?
And who will stand
In the sanctuary of his holiness?
⁴The one clean of hand
And pure of heart.
The one
Who does not
Direct his desire to the emptiness of deceit;
Who does not
Make an oath in order to deceive.
⁵He is the one
Who
Will receive a blessing
From the Lord
And justness from
The God who delivers him.

⁶Such are the people who
Humbly consult with him.

Those who search for you,
My Lord,
Are the true descendants of Jacob.

⁷O gates,
Lift up your heads!
Rise up and open
You gateways of old!
And the King
Of Honor and Abundance
Will come in.
⁸Who is this King
Of Honor and Abundance?

The Lord,
The Mighty One,
The Champion.
The Lord,
Our hero in the struggle.

⁹O gates,
Lift up your heads!
Rise up and open
You gateways of old!
And the King of Glory
Will come in.
¹⁰Who is this King of Glory?

The Lord of Hosts,
The Almighty One,
He is the King of Glory.

# Psalm 25

[1]To you
My Lord,
Will I direct my desire.
[2]My God,
In you I place my trust;
Let me not be ashamed
For having trusted.
Let not my enemies
Exult themselves over me.

[3]Indeed,
All who eagerly look for you
And place their hope in you,
Will not be ashamed.
But,
Those who treacherously depart from you
Are empty handed and will be.

⁴My Lord,
Make the conduct you require known to me.
Teach me the ways you prefer.
⁵Cause me to walk in your faithfulness,
In your truth.
And teach me.
For you are the
God of my deliverance.
Longingly do I wait for you...
All day long.

⁶My Lord,
Remember your mercy and kindness;
For they are from the oldest of days.
⁷Remember not the sins of my youth
Or my wrong doing.
But, remember me according to your graciousness,
On account of your goodness
My Lord,
Not mine.

⁸My Lord is good and just.
Therefore,
He will instruct sinners in the way.
⁹He causes those who worship him
To walk in sound judgment.
And those, the humble,
He teaches his way.

¹⁰All the ways of the Lord
Are of kindness and dependability
To those who respect
And observe his covenant,
His contractual obligations.

¹¹My Lord,
For the sake of your name,
On account of who you are,
Pardon my guilt;
For it is great.

¹²Who is this,
This man who revers the Lord?
He is the one the Lord will instruct
In the way he is to choose.
¹³He, himself, is the one who will rest
In the prosperity of goodness.
And his descendants will
Inherit the earth.

¹⁴The secret conversations of a friend
Belong to those who revere the Lord.
And the Lord
Makes this alliance of friendship known.

¹⁵My eyes are continuously fixed
Upon my Lord.
For it is he who will
Remove my feet from the net;
Even from one in which
I have ensnared myself.

¹⁶Please,
My Lord,
Turn your attention towards me
And be gracious to me;
For I am alone and in need.
¹⁷The anxieties of my heart are extensive;
Lead me out of all my distress.
¹⁸Look with sympathy
On my misery and my trouble
And take away all my sins.
¹⁹Look and see how numerous
Are those hostile to me.
And how they hate me with
An unjust and violent hatred.
²⁰Preserve my life and deliver me.
Let me not be ashamed
For having sought refuge in you.

²¹Integrity of heart
And uprightness of conduct
Will keep watch over me;
Because my hope is in you.

²²And God,
Redeem Israel from all her need
And her sources of distress.

# Psalm 26

¹My Lord,
Judge in my favor.
Because, in you my Lord,
I have trusted without fail.

²Put
Me to
The test,
My Lord,
And try me.
Test with Fire:
My emotions,
My character,
And my mind.
³For your
Kindness and graciousness
Are my focus.
And I have walked, lived
In your continual favor.

⁴I do not keep company with
False, deceptive people.
Nor do I associate with
Pretenders,
Those who craftily conceal
What they really think.
⁵I hate the assembly
That does evil
And I will not keep
Company with wickedness.

⁶I wash my hands in purity
And solemnly approach
Your alter my Lord.
⁷To praise you aloud
With thanksgiving.
And to make known to all,
Your miraculous acts and
Your wonderful judgments.

⁸My Lord,
I love this dwelling
That is your house
And the place where
Your glory can be seen.
⁹Do not remove my soul
With the sinners nor
My life with
The men of blood.
¹⁰The ones in whose hands
Are wickedness and infamy.
And whose hands are full
From accepting bribes.

¹¹But as for me,
I will walk
In innocence with integrity.
Ransom me my Lord;
Redeem me.
Be gracious unto me.

¹²My foot now stands on level ground.
In the assembly of worshipers
I will kneel in adoration of
My Lord.

# Psalm 27

¹The Lord
Is my light and my deliverance;
Of whom shall I be afraid?
The Lord
Is my life's refuge;
Of whom shall I be in dread?

²When those who do evil
Come against me, to tear me apart.
When my adversaries and my enemies
Come against me;
They will stumble and they will fall.
³Though an army of them
Were encamped against me,
In battle formations,
I will not be afraid.
Though they were to
Bring war against me,
Even in this,
I will be confident;
I will trust in my refuge.

⁴One thing
Have I asked from
My Lord.
The one thing
That I seek from him
Is to remain
In the household of
My Lord;
To dwell in his presence
All the days of my life.
To behold the kindness of
My Lord
And to contemplate and reflect
Upon him in his temple.
⁵For, in the day of misery,
He will hide me
In the protection of his tent.
He will lift me
High upon a rock,
He will set me
In a place of safety and refuge.
⁶And then I will overshadow
My enemies that surround me.
And with shouts of joy
I will sacrifice
An offering of thanksgiving
In his tent.
I will sing, yes,
I will play music
And sing praises to
My Lord.

⁷My Lord,
Hear my voice
And accept my request;
I call upon you.
Be gracious to me, favor me,
And respond to my request.
On your behalf,
⁸My heart has said,
"Call on me."
My Lord,
It is to you that I call.
⁹Do not withdraw
Your favor from me.
Do not, in anger,
Turn your servant away.
For you alone are my help.
Do not give up on me
Or abandon me,
God of my deliverance.
¹⁰For, if my father and my mother
Were to abandon me
Still will my Lord
Care for me.

¹¹My Lord,
Teach me your way.
Lead me
In the even way
That leads to life.
For the sake of
My watchful enemies.

¹²Do not surrender me
To my passionate enemies.
For there have appeared against me
Witnesses who swear to falsehood.
And their witness is violence.
¹³If I had not believed
And gained an understanding of
The goodness of my Lord
In the land of the living....

¹⁴Wait
With your mind turned
Towards our Lord.
Be courageous and confident.
And be strong in your heart.
Yes, look eagerly and
Wait.
With your mind focused
On our Lord.

# Psalm 28

¹My Lord,
To you I will call.
My Rock,
Do not be deaf to me.
Lest, if you turn away from me
And are silent,
I become like....
Like those who sink
Into the world of the dead.
²Hear my cries
As I plead for mercy.
Hear the sound of
My desperate pleading;
As I repeatedly scream out
To you for help.
As I raise my hands towards your
Holiest sanctuary.

³Do not carry me off
With those who are wicked,
Those who practice injustice.
Who speak peaceably,
As a friend with their neighbors,
While harboring evil intent in their hearts.

⁴Reward them,
According
To what they have done
And according
To the evil of their deeds.
According
To the enterprise of their hands,
Reward them.
Cause their actions
To turn against them;
Give them the retribution
They have earned.

⁵Because they will not pay attention
To the actions of the Lord
Or to the enterprise
Of his hands.
He will cast them down and
Their households will not flourish;
He will not restore them.

⁶Praised and adored is
My Lord.
For he has heard
My pleas for mercy.
⁷The Lord
Is my refuge and protection,
The one in whom
My heart trusts.
I am helped
And I am ecstatic
And with my song
I will praise him.

⁸The Lord
Is the refuge to his people.
The mountain stronghold,
The help
To his anointed one.

⁹Deliver your people
And bless Israel,
Your inheritance.
Tend to them.
Shepherd them.
Maintain them forever.

# Psalm 29

¹Give recognition to the Lord,
O sons of The Almighty.
Give recognition to the Lord's
Honor and might.
²Give recognition to the Lord,
To the glory of his name.

Worship the Lord
In his holy splendor.

³The voice of the Lord
Is upon the waters.
The glory of the Lord
Thunders.
The Lord is over the seas.
⁴The voice of the Lord
In Power.
The voice of the Lord
In majesty.

⁵The voice of the Lord
Shatters the cedars.
Yes, the Lord
Destroys the mighty cedars of Lebanon.
⁶He makes the cedars of Lebanon...
Appear to skip like a calf.
And the mountain of Sirion,
Like a young wild bull.

⁷The voice of the Lord
Cleaves the sky with flames of fire.
⁸The voice of the Lord
Causes the wilderness to tremble.
The Lord
Causes the wilderness of Kadesh to tremble.
⁹The voice of the Lord
Causes the mighty oaks
To writhe in anguish
And lays the forest bare.

And everything in the world,
His temple,
Declares, "Glory!"

¹⁰The Lord sits enthroned
Over the torrential storm.
And the Lord will sit enthroned,
King forever.

¹¹The Lord will give
Strength and protection to his people.
The Lord will bless
His people with peace.

# Psalm 30

[1]My Lord,
I will exalt and praise you.
For You have
Drawn me up from the depths.
And you have not
Allowed my enemies
To rejoice over my death.
[2]My Lord,
My God,
I called out to you for help
And you healed me.
[3]My Lord,
You have brought me back
From the edge of death itself.
You have brought me back
To life from amongst those
Descending into the world of the dead.

⁴O you, his faithful ones,
Sing to the Lord!
And give thankful praise
At the mention of his holiness!

⁵In his anger,
For a moment.
In his favor,
For a lifetime.
Weeping may stay
While it is evening.
But to the morning
Belongs rejoicing.

⁶As for me,
When I was living at ease
I had a false sense of security.
I said,
"I have made it!
Nothing will ever touch me now."

⁷My Lord,
It was in your good pleasure,
In the favor that you showed me,
That you caused my life of ease.
I made it
My strong and fortified mountain.
Yet when you hid your face,
When you withdrew your favor,
I was horrified.
As my security,
My mountain,
Crumbled.

⁸To you my Lord I will call.
And it is to you,
The only Lord,
That I will implore
For compassion.

⁹I called out to you,
"How do you gain anything
From my blood being so cruelly shed?
In my going down to the grave,
Going down into the pit?
Will the dust in my grave praise and worship you?
Will it explain your truth and faithfulness?
¹⁰My Lord, Hear me!
My Lord, be gracious to me!
Be the one who helps me."

¹¹And you changed my funeral
Into my dance.
You removed my garments of mourning
And surrounded me with joy.

¹²So now, my honor,
All that is noble within me,
Will praise you
And it will not be silent.
My Lord,
My God,
I will give thanks
In praise of you...
Forever.

# Psalm 31

¹In you, my Lord,
I have taken refuge.
For that,
Never let me be put to shame.
In your righteousness,
In your justness,
Save me.
²Bend your ear to me
And listen.
Hasten and snatch me away;
Deliver me.
Be to me...
As a mountain refuge,
As the fortified dwelling
Of a mountain stronghold,
And save me.

³For you are my mountain stronghold
And the protective cliffs it sits upon.
And, on account of your name,
You will lead me
Through the wilderness
And escort me
To a place of rest.
⁴You will free me from the trap
Which has been covertly set against me.
For you are my protection,
You are my refuge.
⁵Into your hands
I will entrust my spirit.
For you have redeemed
My pledge to you.
My Lord,
The God who is faithful.

⁶I hate the devotions made
To the vanities of nothingness,
To the idols of things
That do not really exist.

But as for me,
I trust in my Lord.

⁷I will shout in exultation
And rejoice in your faithfulness,
In your goodness.
Because,
You have looked after my afflictions
⁸And you have not
Placed me
In the controlling hands
Of my enemy.
You have
Put my feet down
In an open space,
A place of safety
And of security.

⁹Be gracious to me, my Lord.
For, even so,
I am depressed and worried.
My eyes are darkened from vexation.
My body and soul are swollen in grief.
¹⁰In grief
My life has stopped.
And my years...
Now end in groaning.
Because of my misery,
My strength falters
And my bones begin to decay.

¹¹On account of my adversaries
I have become a disgrace.
And to my neighbors...
Exceedingly so.
And an object of dread
To my acquaintances.
Those seeing me on the street
Flee from me.

¹²I am forgotten.
I am gone from the mind,
As one who is dead.
I have become...
Like a broken utensil.

¹³For I hear
The whispered reports of many.
Terror from every side
As they are conspiring
Altogether against me.
They plan the evil
Of taking my life.

¹⁴But I,
I trust in you, my Lord.
I still say,
"You are my God."
¹⁵What happens to me
Is in your hands.
Please,
Deliver me
From the hands of my enemies.
Deliver me
From the hands of those who are
Hostile to me
And
From the hands of those who
Pursue and persecute me.

¹⁶Let your face shine
Upon your servant.
By your favor,
Save me.

¹⁷My Lord,
Do not let me be put to shame,
For I have called upon you.
Let the wicked be put to shame.
Let them go crying for the grave.

¹⁸Let the lips,
Which do falsely swear and accuse,
Be bound with silence.
Those lips,
Which are speaking brazenly
About the righteous;
Those,
Speaking in arrogance
And with contempt.

¹⁹How abundant are your blessings!
The ones which you have stored up
For those who honor you.
The ones which you,
In the plain sight of everyone,
Have performed for
And bestowed upon
Those who are taking refuge in you.

²⁰You hide them,
In the protection of your presence,
From the conspiracies of men.
You shelter them, as in a hut,
From contentious tongues.

²¹Praised be Our Lord!
For he has shown
His marvelous concern;
He has shown
His faithfulness to me
In a city of distress.

²²Alarmed and in haste I said,
"I am cut off from you.
I have been removed from your sight,
Out of your sight and out of your mind."
But you did hear
The sound of my desperate pleading
When I cried out to you for help.

²³Now all of you,
His faithful ones,
Love our Lord!
For our Lord
Keeps watch over the faithful.
And he exceedingly rewards,
According to their own actions,
Those acting arrogantly.

²⁴Be strong, be confident!
And let your heart show its strength.
Let it show courage.
All of you
Who wait for and hope in
Our Lord.

# Psalm 32

[1] Happy is he
Whose transgressions are
Taken away;
Whose sin is
Forgiven.
[2] Happy is the man
To whom the Lord
Does not attribute guilt.
And in whose spirit
There is no deception.

³Because I kept silent
About my sin,
My bones became weakened.
My body... worn out
By my screaming all day long
In defiance and distress.
⁴For continually,
By day and by night,
Your presence weighed
Heavily upon me.
I was like sweet cream
Turned
By the heat of the day.

⁵But then,

I conceded.
I told you about my sin
And I did not conceal
My guiltiness.
I concealed nothing.
I said,
"I will confess all
My transgressions
To my Lord."
And you did take away
The guilt of my sin.

⁶Because of this,
Let the faithful pray to you
In the moment of finding sin.
Then these many flood waters
Will not befall them.
⁷For you are my protection.
You keep me from this stress
As you have protectively moved
Shields of deliverance around me.

⁸I will instruct you.
I will teach you the way
In which you are to walk.
I plan to watch over you.
⁹Do not be
Like a horse or a mule;
In which there is no understanding.
Whose strength must be restrained
With a bridle and a reign;
Because it will not approach you.

¹⁰Many are the pains of the wicked.
But for the one trusting in the Lord,
Merciful faithfulness
Protectively surrounds him.

¹¹Rejoice in our Lord!
You who are righteous,
Shout in jubilation!
Begin to sing exultantly,
All you who are upright in heart!

# Psalm 33

¹Devout ones,
Rejoice in our Lord.
Belt out your cries of jubilation
In praise of your Lord.
To the upright,
That is a proper and fitting
Song of praise.
²Praise our Lord with a lyre!
Play for him
On a harp of ten strings!
³Sing for him a new song!
Play beautifully on the strings
And loudly shout in jubilation!

⁴For the word of our Lord
Is just.
And all his work is done
In faithfulness.
⁵Loving honesty, loyalty,
Fair decisions, and justice;
Our Lord has filled the earth
With his graciousness and mercy.

⁶By the word of our Lord
The heavens were created.
And by the breath of his mouth,
All their hosts;
The sun, the moon, and
All the heavenly bodies.
⁷He then gathered the waters of the sea
As though into a bottle.
Placing the primeval flood
As though into a storehouse.
⁸Let all the earth
Tremble before our Lord.
Let all those who
Dwell in the world
Stand in awe
Before him.
⁹For he spoke
And the earth came into being.
He gave the order
And the land stood forth.

¹⁰Our Lord suspends
The purposes of the nations;
He frustrates
The plans of the peoples.
¹¹But
The purpose of our Lord
Will remain standing forever;
The plans of his heart...
For all generations.

¹²Happy is the nation
Whose God is the Lord.
For he has chosen its people
To be separated unto himself;
To be his heritage,
To be his legacy.

¹³Our Lord looks from heaven
And sees all people.
¹⁴From the place where he dwells,
He observes and considers
All those dwelling on the earth.
¹⁵He sees what is forming in their hearts
And gives consideration to all they do.
¹⁶The king is not made victorious
By the greatness of his army.
A valiant hero is not saved
By his great power and ability.
¹⁷It is a deception
To place hope for victory
In the horse.
Nor can you rely on it
As a means of escape,
Even with its great strength.

¹⁸Behold,
The eye of our Lord
Is turned towards those
Who revere him.
His attention,
Towards those who wait
For his faithful mercy.
¹⁹This, in order to pull their soul
Away from death's door;
To preserve their life
During times of great hunger.

[20] Every fiber of our being
Waits for our Lord.
He is
Our strength
And our protection.
[21] For in him
Our heart rejoices;
For in his holy name
We have trusted.

[22] My Lord,
Let your faithful mercy
Be upon us.
Even as we wait for
And place our hope in
You.

# Psalm 34

¹At all times
And on every occasion,
I will bless and praise my Lord.
The song of his praise
Will continuously be in my heart.
²My soul will boast of my Lord.
And those
Bowed before him in worship
Will hear, rejoice, and be merry.

³With me,
Praise and honor our Lord!
Together
Let us speak highly of his name.

⁴I sought my Lord in prayer
And he answered me.
And from all my objects of dread
He has delivered me.
⁵Those with me
Have looked confidently to him.
And they shine forth with joy,
They are radiant,
And they are not ashamed.

⁶This afflicted man
Cried out
And his Lord heard.
And from all of his distress,
His Lord has saved him.

⁷The angel of our Lord
Encamps as a guard,
Encircling those who
Revere and honor him.
And he will rescue them.

⁸Perceive, by experience,
And understand
That our Lord is good.
Happy is the one
Who will take refuge in him.

⁹You holy ones of the Lord,
Honor your Lord!
For those honoring him
Lack nothing.
¹⁰Even young lions
Are often food poor and hungry.
But those who worshipfully
Seek our Lord in prayer
Will not lack
Any truly good thing.

¹¹Come children,
Listen to me!
I will teach you
The religion of our Lord.

¹²Who is the man who desires life?
Who loves the days, so that
He may get to know
What is good?
You?
Then,
¹³Guard your tongue
From evil
And your lips
From speaking deceit.
¹⁴Turn aside from evil
And do good.
Aim at and
Practice peace;
Pursue it.

¹⁵The eyes of our Lord
Are turned towards
The righteous,
The innocent.
The ears of our Lord
Towards
Their cries for help.

¹⁶But the face of our Lord
Is turned against
Those who do evil.
They will be forgotten
As he causes
Even the memory of them
To perish from the earth.

¹⁷The righteous
Cry out for help
And our Lord
Hears.
And he delivers them
From all their distress.

¹⁸Our Lord is near
To the brokenhearted.
And he rescues
The crushed in spirit.

¹⁹The deprivations
Of the righteous
Are many,
But
Our Lord
Will deliver him
From all of them.

²⁰He is protecting all of his bones.
Not one of them has been broken.

²¹Evil will slay the wicked,
The guilty.
And those hating the innocent
Will suffer
For their own guilt.

²²But
Our Lord ransoms
The life of his servants
From this evil.
All those taking refuge
In him
Will have no guilt
From which to suffer.

# Psalm 35

¹My Lord,
In your court,
Carry on against my opponents.
Fight those who are fighting me.
²Arm yourself,
Seize both shield and buckler
And rise up in my support.
³Make ready the spear
And block their path
And shout your challenge
To those pursuing me.
Declare to me,
"I am your help;
I am your deliverance."

⁴Let those
Seeking to take my life,
Be put to shame.
Let them be humiliated.
Let those
Planning my misfortune...
Let them be turned back.
Let them be mortified
And let them flee.

⁵Let them become like the chaff
Before the wind.
With the angel of the Lord,
Who is the wind,
Pushing them all the way.
⁶Let their path become
Dark, confusing, and slippery.
With the angel of the Lord,
Who is the wind,
Pursuing them on their way.

⁷For, without cause,
They secretly set
A trap for me
With their net.
Without cause,
They dug and concealed
A pit for me.

⁸Let ruin come upon them;
Without their being aware
Of its approach.
And the net,
Which they secretly set,
Let it entrap them.
Let them fall into it,
To their ruin.

⁹And my soul
Will shout with exultation
In my Lord.
It will rejoice
In his help,
In his deliverance.

¹⁰All of my being,
The very core of who I am,
Will say,
"My Lord,
Who is like you?
Delivering the weak
And the afflicted
From the one
Who is too strong for him.
Delivering the weak
And the one in need
From the one
Who is robbing him."

¹¹False witnesses appear in court
And testify against me.
They cross-examine me
Concerning things...
About which
I know nothing.

¹²In exchange for good
They have rewarded me
With evil.
To me...
This has been like
Being bereft of a child.

¹³But, as for me.
When they were sick
My garment was sackcloth,
The garment of sorrow.
I humbled myself with fasting.
And when my prayers
Came back unanswered,
¹⁴I behaved like a friend.
Like they were one of my brothers.
Like unto the mourning of a mother,
I bowed low in self neglect;
Mourning for them.

¹⁵But when I stumbled,
They gathered together and rejoiced.
They became strangers
Whom I did not know.
And they tore me to pieces
With their words;
And they will not be silent.
¹⁶They are profane and
Godless court jesters.
Ones who gnash at me
With their teeth.

¹⁷My Lord,
For how long
Will you idly watch?
Restore my life
From their roaring deceptions.
From these virile young lions,
Rescue my suffering soul.

¹⁸I will worshipfully praise you
In the great congregation;
The one assembled
To worship you.
With that people,
Mighty in number,
I will praise you.

¹⁹Do not let my fraudulent enemies
Maliciously rejoice over me.
Nor let those who
Hate me without cause,
Wink their eye at me
In mockery.
²⁰For they speak not
Of peace and friendship.
No,
Rather they scheme
And plan matters
Which are full of
Fraud and deceit,
Against those living
Peaceably and quietly in the land.

²¹And they open
Their mouths wide
Against me.
Saying,
"Aha, aha!
Our eyes have seen it!"

²²But
My Lord,
It is you who have seen.
Do not be deaf
To what they are saying.
Do not be silent.
My Lord,
Do not be distant
From me.

²³Arise and put things in motion.
Awaken your purpose
To judge my case.
My God
And
My Lord,
Awaken your purpose
Towards settling my dispute.

$^{24}$My Lord,
My God,
Pass judgment for me
According to
Your honesty,
Your loyalty,
Your knowledge of
What is right.
Do not let them
Maliciously rejoice over me.
$^{25}$Do not let them say,
In their hearts,
"Aha!
Just what our souls
Have long desired!"
Do not let them say,
"We have engulfed
And ruined him!"

$^{26}$Let all those who
Rejoice at my misfortune
And distress
Be put to shame.
Let them be ashamed
Of what they have done.
Let all those who
Do great wrongs against me,
Who try to elevate
Their significance by
Being against me,
Let them be clothed in shame
And public disgrace.

²⁷But,
Let all those who take delight
In justice being done for me,
Let them give
A ringing shout of jubilation!
Let them rejoice!
And let them continuously say,
"Great is our Lord!
The one who takes delight in
The peace and well-being
Of his servant."

²⁸And my tongue will proclaim
Your loyalty,
Your justness,
Your righteousness.
All day, every day,
It will sing your praise.

# Psalm 36

[1]Deep within,
My heart prophesies
Against the wicked, sin,
And transgression.
Saying,
"Never mind reverence and awe,
The wicked do not even have
A dread of God.
For their eyes do not see
What is before them."

²For his tongue deals
Smoothly with himself.
It creates an image
That is good
In his own eyes.
He is blinded
And not able to detect
The guilt of his iniquity.
He is not able to hate it.

³The words coming
Out of his mouth
Are full of nothingness and sorrow,
Full of fraud and deceit.
He has ceased having insight
And from acting prudently.
He has ceased from speaking well
And from doing what is right.

⁴He plans injustice and trouble
While lying upon his bed.
He takes his stand
Upon a path...
That is not good.
Evil...
He does not refuse.

⁵My Lord,
Your graciousness
Is so vast
It extends to the heavens.
Your faithfulness
To the clouds above.
⁶Your justness and loyalty
Are like the mightiest of mountains.
Your decisions and judgments
Are like the deepest of the seas.

My Lord,
It is you who saves
Both man and beast
From danger.

⁷My God,
Your graciousness is
Very valuable and
Dearly precious.
Indeed,
Your people take refuge in this.
This is
Your protection.
This is
The shadow of your wings.

⁸They will be filled
And refreshed
From the abundance
Of your house.
And you will give them drink
From the strong and deep river
That is your bliss.

⁹For with you,
My Lord,
Is the source...
The fountain of
All life and living.
For it is with your light
That we will see light.
It is in you that we know
What living truly means.

¹⁰Stretch out your graciousness
Over those
Who know you.
And your justness and loyalty
Over those
Who are upright in heart.

¹¹Do not let
The foot of the arrogant
Tread me down.
Do not let
The hand of the wicked
Make me homeless.

¹²There they are,
Those who practice
Deception and injustice.
They have fallen prostrate.
They have been
Thrust down and overthrown.
And they are not able
To rise up again.

# Psalm 37

<sup>1</sup>Do not excite yourself
Or become vexed
At the success
Of those doing evil.
Do not be agitated
Or become envious
At the prosperity
Of those doing unjust things.
<sup>2</sup>For like the grass,
They will hastily
Dry up and wither.
Like the greenery of springtime,
They will wither
And fall to the ground.

<sup>3</sup>Do good.
Do what is right
And trust in our Lord.
Live calmly and securely in the land
And practice faithfulness.
<sup>4</sup>Find your pleasure
In our Lord
And he will grant you
The desires of your heart.

⁵Roll onto the shoulders
Of our Lord
All your concern;
For your life and
For the path you must take.
Rely on him
And he will act
On your behalf.
⁶And he will make known
His justice for you.
As if with a bright light,
He will make it known.
And his judgment for your case,
As if displayed
Under the noonday sun.

⁷Be still
And be quiet
Before our Lord.
And wait for him.
Do not excite yourself
Or become vexed
With the one
Who is successful
While on his unjust path;
With the one
Who carries out
Wicked plots and schemes.

⁸Let anger alone
And leave rage behind.
Do not excite yourself
Or become vexed.
Which only leads to
Harm and evil.
⁹For those doing evil
And bringing harm
Will be cut off from
Our Lord.
They will perish
From the land.
But those who wait for
And hope in
Our Lord,
They will inherit
The earth.

¹⁰For, in just a little while,
The wicked will be no more.
They will have vanished from the land.
And though you carefully
Examine and search his place,
He will not be found.
He will not be.
¹¹But those who are humble,
Those who bow before our Lord,
They will inherit the earth.
And will take great delight
In his deliverance,
In his abundance of
Peace,
Prosperity,
And contentment.

¹²The wicked plan evil schemes
Against the innocent,
Against the devout.
And they grind their teeth
In rage towards him.
¹³But our Lord
Is not troubled by their schemes.
He knows
They are not worth
Excitement or vexation.
For he knows
That the day appointed
For the wicked
Is approaching.

¹⁴The wicked have drawn
Their sword
And they have bent
Their bow.
To bring destruction to
The poor in spirit
And to those
In need of justice.
To ruthlessly kill
Those of strong moral character,
Those who are blameless
In their conduct.
¹⁵But
The sword of the wicked
Will return home
To their own heart
And their bow will be broken.

¹⁶Better is the little
Belonging to the upright
Than the wealth
Of much wickedness.
Do not become vexed.
¹⁷For the arms,
The strength,
Of wickedness
Will be shattered.
But our Lord
Sustains
Moral innocence.

[18] Our Lord knows
The days appointed
To the impeccable,
To those having integrity;
And their inheritance
Is forever.
[19] They will not be put to shame
In times of evil.
And in days of famine and hunger,
They will eat their fill and be satisfied.

[20] But all wickedness
Will perish.
And the enemies of our Lord,
Those who practice wickedness,
Are like the noble splendor
Of the meadows.
They will fade away.
Like so much smoke,
They will vanish.

[21] Wickedness borrows
And does not pay it back.
But the innocent and upright
Is gracious, shows favor,
And is giving.
[22] Yes, those
Blessed by our Lord
Will inherit the earth.
But those
Placed under a curse by him
Will be cut off.

²³The steps of a man,
Even the young and the strong,
Are made ready
By our Lord.
And he takes pleasure in
And is delighted by
Walking this path.
²⁴And though he will
Encounter disaster,
He will not be hurled down;
He will not be undone.
For our Lord
Is holding and supporting
His hand.

²⁵I was once a young boy
And now I have grown old.
In all that time,
I have not seen
The innocent and upright
Abandoned.
I have not seen him
Left in need.
Nor his children
Left
Searching and pleading
For bread.
²⁶He is ever gracious
And showing favor
To the poor and needy.
And he lends freely.
And his children
Come into blessing.

²⁷Change your direction
And turn away from evil.
Do good.
Do what is right
And live calmly and securely in the land,
Forevermore.
²⁸For our Lord loves justice
And will not abandon
The ones faithful to him.
He, forevermore,
Guards and cares for them.
But the children of the guilty...
Will be cut off.
²⁹But
The just, the innocent,
Those who are faithful,
They will inherit the land
And will dwell upon it
Forevermore.

³⁰The mouth of the faithful
Will proclaim prudence and wisdom.
And his tongue will speak
What is right and just.
³¹All of the teachings,
All the instructions,
Of his God
Are in his heart.
He loves them
And muses on them
Day and night.
And his steps
Do not falter.

³²The guilty and wicked person
Lies in wait
For the faithful innocent.
Seeking
To put him to death.
³³But
Our Lord will not leave him
In the power or the purposes
Of the wicked.
And
Our Lord will not condemn the faithful
When he is so judged by the wicked.

³⁴Trust in and wait for
Our Lord.
Hold onto
And devote yourself to
His way.
And he will exalt you;
He will raise you up
To inherit and possess the land.
You will, in triumph, watch
The disappearance of the wicked.

³⁵I have seen the wickedness of a man,
Violent, exposed, and spreading
Like a tree of luxuriant leaves
Growing in its native soil.
³⁶He went his way
And lo,
He has vanished from the land.
And though I have searched for him,
He could not be found.

³⁷Keep watch over
Purity and innocence.
Shepherd and protect
Honesty and uprightness.
For such a man,
The future outcome
Will be peace.
³⁸But
Those who are being disloyal,
Who are transgressing...
They will altogether
Be destroyed.
For the wicked,
The future outcome
Is to be cut off;
To perish from the land.

³⁹But the deliverance of the faithful,
From trouble and wickedness,
Is from our Lord.
Who is their stronghold,
The place of their refuge,
In times of need and distress.
⁴⁰And our Lord will help them.
He will bring them
Into security;
He will deliver them
From the wickedness.
And he will help and save them
Because
They have taken refuge in him.

# Psalm 38

¹My Lord,
Do not punish me in your anger;
Do not rebuke me in your rage.
²For your arrows
Have penetrated into me.
And your hand
Has descended upon me.
³My body has no health
Because of
Your indignation,
Your displeasure,
Over my mistreatment of you.
My bones have no peace
Because of
My sin.

⁴For my guilt
And its consequences
Have overpowered me.
Like a heavy burden,
One too heavy
For me to bear.
⁵My wounds
Have started to stink
As they begin to rot and fester.
Because of my folly,
Because of
My foolishness.

⁶I am twisted
In irritation.
I am exceedingly
Bent out of shape
By this illness.
All day long
I move about
Dressed in grief,
Both
Dirty and unkempt.
⁷For my insides are filled
With a burning inflammation.
And there is no health in my body.
⁸I am powerless
And faint
And I am greatly crushed.
I am roaring about my distress
From the growling of my heart.

⁹My Lord,
My Sovereign,
All my longings
Are before you
And in plain sight.
And my groaning
Is not hidden
From your view.
¹⁰My heart races irregularly.
My strength and good health
Have forsaken me.
And the light of my eyes,
It has also gone from me.
Those who love me,
¹¹My friends and companions,
Remove themselves from my afflictions.
And those closest to me,
My family,
Keep their distance from me.
Those seeking to destroy my life...
¹²Lay their snares.
And those intent upon
Doing me harm,
Speak in threats,
And promise me
Destruction.
All day long
They plot fraud and treachery.

¹³But I am
Like one who is deaf,
I do not hear these things.
And I am like one who is mute,
Who does not open his mouth.
¹⁴Yes, I am
Like a man
Who does not hear these things.
And in whose mouth
There are no responsive retorts.
¹⁵For I wait for you
My Lord.
You will reply,
My sovereign,
My God.
¹⁶For as I have said,
"Lest those who make themselves great
At my expense
Maliciously rejoice over me,
In the slipping of my foot."

[17] For I am ready
To stumble and fall.
And my pain is ever with me.
For I admit my guilt;
[18] I confess my sin.
From my sin
I am anxious.

[19] And those who are
Treating me as an enemy
Are alive and well.
Indeed, they are countless in number.
[20] Yes, many are my personal enemies
Who hate me wrongfully,
Those who oppose me with lies.
My adversaries are those
Who reward evil and misery
Instead of what is good;
Instead of my pursuit of the good.

[21] Do not abandon me
My Lord.
Do not be distant from me
My God.
[22] Hurry to be my help
My sovereign Lord,
My deliverance.

# Psalm 39

¹I have said,
"I will protect my ways
From missing the mark
With my tongue.
I will restrain my mouth
With a muzzle
While the wicked
Are yet before me."

²I tied my tongue
With silence.
I was silent
But to no avail.
And my pain
Was stirred up.
³My heart became warm within me.
While sighing in prayer
A fire began to burn.
Then with my tongue
I spoke.

⁴My Lord,
Make known to me my end.
What is the measured limit of my days?
And let me know
How transient I am.
⁵Behold, you have set my days;
Mere moments.
And the duration of my life
Is like nothing
Before you.

Indeed,
Complete meaningless vanity
Is the position of
Everyman.

⁶Indeed,
As mere empty images,
As dark and gloomy shadows,
People move to and fro.
Yes,
In vain,
To no purpose,
They bustle about
Pouring their wealth
Into a big heap.
Not knowing
Who will gather it
To themselves
In the end.

⁷And now,
My Lord,
What do I hope for?
My hope is in you.
⁸Remove me
From all my transgressions.
Please, do not make me
The taunt of the foolish.

⁹I am silenced.
My mouth
I will not open.
For it is you
Who has done this.

¹⁰Remove your affliction
From upon me.
While your hand
Moves against me,
I am undone.

¹¹With reproach against sin,
You chastise a man.
You dissolve him
As a moth
Does to loveliness.

Indeed,
Complete meaningless vanity
Is the position of
Everyman.

[12] My Lord,
Please hear my prayer.
And please heed
My cry for help.
Please do not be silent at my tears,
Do not be deaf to my weeping.
For in your company
I am a new comer without rights,
One who is in need of protection.
A resident alien,
Like all of my ancestors before me.
[13] Spare me,
Turn the anger in your eyes
Away from me.
Remove your reproach.
That I may become
Cheerful once again;
Before I die
And am no more.

# Psalm 40

¹I waited,
Waited for my Lord.
And he heard
My cry for help.
²He reached down
To me and pulled me up
From out of the wasteland world
Of the dying,
From out of its mud and mire.
And he placed my feet
Upon solid rock,
Making my steps steady.
³And he set in my mouth
A fresh new song,
A song of praise to our God.
Many will see and honor
And trust in our Lord.

⁴Happy is the man
Who has made the Lord
The object of his trust.
And who has not turned his trust
Towards the arrogant enemies.
Or towards those who have turned
Towards the way of the lie.

⁵You,
My Lord,
My God,
You have made
And given effect to
Many wonderful
And miraculous acts.
If I tried to proclaim them,
To try and speak about them...
They are too numerous
To recount.
And you give us much thought.
There is none to compare to you.

⁶You have not taken pleasure in
Sacrifice and food offerings.
You have dug out my ears
And opened my understanding.
You have not demanded mere
Whole burnt offerings and sin offerings.
⁷Then I said,
"See, I have come in
With the scroll of the book
That is written for me.
My God,
⁸I take delight in
The doing of your will.
And your law
Is at the very center
Of my being."
⁹I have announced
The good news of deliverance
In the great assembly.
Behold, my lips
I have not restrained.
This,
My Lord,
You know.

¹⁰I have not concealed your justness
Within the confines of my heart.
I have praised your trustworthiness
And the deliverance you have provided.
I have not concealed
Your graciousness or your constancy
From the great assembly.
¹¹You,
My Lord,
You will not restrain
Your compassionate mercy
From me.
Your graciousness and
Your constancy
Will continuously watch over me.

¹²For distress and suffering
Have completely surrounded me,
Until they are beyond measure.
The guilt of my iniquities
Has overtaken me.
And I am not able to see clearly...
They are more numerous than
The hairs of my head.
And my courage has forsaken me.

¹³My Lord,
Let it please you
To deliver me.
My Lord,
Hurry to help me.

¹⁴Let those who
Strive to take my life away
Be put to shame and
Be altogether mortified.
Let those who
Desire my injury
Be ashamed.
¹⁵Let those who say to me,
"Aha, aha!"
Be appalled at themselves
As the wages
Of their shame.

¹⁶Let all who search for you
Rejoice.
And let them rejoice
In you.
Let those who love your help
Continuously say,
"Our Lord is great!"

¹⁷But as for me,
I am poor, wretched, and needy.
My Lord and Sovereign
Will devise a plan for me.
My God,
You are my help
And my deliverer;
Please...
Do not delay.

# Psalm 41

[1] O the happiness and blessings
Belonging to the one
Who keeps an eye
Towards the helpless.
In the day of evil and misery,
Our Lord will deliver him.
[2] Our Lord
Will protect and keep him alive.
In the land, he will be called happy.
And our Lord will not surrender him
To the cravings of his enemies.
[3] Our Lord
Sustains and supports him
Upon his couch of illness.

⁴And for my part,
I have said,
"My Lord,
Favor me;
Be gracious
And heal my soul.
For it is against you
That I have sinned."
⁵My enemies speak evil
Towards me saying,
"When will he die
And his name
Become lost to memory?"
⁶And if one has come
To see for himself,
He speaks empty, worthless words.
His heart collects up any hint
Of my looming disaster, for itself,
And then he goes out
And spreads it in the street.

⁷All those who hate me,
As an enemy,
Whisper together against me.
Against me...
To devise and plan
Evil and misery for me.
They whisper,
⁸"A wicked illness
Has been poured out
Upon him;
He has been anointed.
And where he has lain down,
He will not arise from again."
⁹Yes,
Even a man of my peace,
A good friend,
One in whom I trusted,
One with whom I have
Shared my bread,
Has insidiously
Turned against me.

¹⁰But you
My Lord,
Please favor me; be gracious.
Raise me up again
That I may reward them
Properly.

¹¹By this I understand
That you are delighted with me.
That my enemies are not
Rejoicing in triumph
Over me.

¹²And for my part,
You have taken hold in me,
In my integrity and innocence.
And you have placed me before your face...
Forever.

¹³Praised and adored
Is our Lord,
The God of Israel.
From before time began
And after time ends.
Amen and amen!
This is certain,
This is so!

# Book 2
## Psalms 42-72

# Psalm 42

¹As a deer will crave
The coolest streams of water
That flow in the deepest valleys;
So too, my soul craves you,
My God.
²My soul thirsts for God,
For the God who lives.
When will I go in
And appear before
The presence of God?
Both day and night
³My tears have
Become to me...
My food.
While saying to me,
All day long,
"Where is your God?"

⁴I will remember these things
Even as I will pour out
That which is within me;
As I pour out my soul.
I will remember
That I will go,
Undertaking the processional walk,
To the house of my God;
Among the multitude,
Among the sounds of jubilation
And songs of praise,
Among the roar of a multitude
In celebration.

⁵So, why, my soul
Will you sink down and dissolve?
And why
Will you be turbulently restless
Against me?
Wait for God.
For still I will praise him
For the help of his presence.

⁶My God,
Against me, my soul
Sinks down and dissolves.
Therefore,
I will remember you
From the lands of
Jordan and Hermon
And from the little mountain.
I will remember you
While far from your house.

⁷Even as deluge
Is calling out to deluge,
All to the sound
Of your cascading torrents.
As all of your breaking waves
And large surging waves
Sweep over me.

⁸By day
My Lord will send
His faithful graciousness
And by night
His song will be with me;
A prayer
To the God of my life.
⁹I will say to my God,
My rock,
"For what reason
Have you forgotten me?
For what reason
Will I walk around
In great sorrow,
While oppressed by
Those being hostile?"

¹⁰My adversaries taunt me
While saying,
"Where is your God?"
And it is like
The breaking of my bones.

¹¹But, why, my soul,
Will you sink down and dissolve?
And why
Will you be turbulently restless
Against me?
Wait for God.
For still I will praise him;
For he is my help and salvation.
He is my God.

# Psalm 43

¹My God,
Please...
Render a judgment
In my favor.
And on my behalf
Carry on your lawsuit
Before an unfaithful
And ungodly people.
Save me from the men of
Treachery and injustice.

²For you,
My God,
Are my fortress,
My refuge.
So, why have you rejected me?
For what reason
Must I go about
With my soul darkened
By grief and mourning,
In the oppression of
My enemy?

³Commission your light
And your faithfulness;
Send them!
Cause them to conduct me,
Cause them to bring me
To your holy mountain
And to the places
Where you dwell.

⁴And I will come
To the alter of My God;
To God,
The joy of my rejoicing.
And with music I will praise you
God,
My God.

⁵Why, my soul,
Will you sink down and dissolve?
And why
Will you be turbulently restless
Against me?
Wait for God.
For still I will praise him;
For he is my help and salvation.
He is my God.

# Psalm 44

¹God,
With our own ears we have heard.
Our fathers have proclaimed
The deeds of deliverance
Which you performed
In their day,
In our earliest and
Most ancient of days.
²You,
By the strength of your hand,
You dispossessed the nations
And planted our ancestors
In the land.
You shattered the nations
And set our forebears free.

³For not with their own sword
Did they take possession of the land.
And the strength of their own arm
Did not save them.
For it was the strength of
Your right hand
And the strength of
Your own arm
And the light of
Your presence;
For you were favorable to them.

⁴You are the one,
My king,
My God,
Who both commands
And sends
The help of Jacob.
⁵With your help
We will push back
Our enemies.
In the strength of your name
We will trample
Those rising against us.

⁶For I will not trust
In my bow.
And my sword
Will not save me.
⁷For it is you
Who has saved us
From our foes.
And those who hate us,
You have put to shame.
⁸In God we offer praise;
We have boasted of his greatness
Each and every day.
And your name,
My Lord,
We will praise forever.

⁹But you have rejected
And humiliated us.
And you have not gone out
With our armies.
¹⁰You have caused us
To be turned back by the enemy;
To be repelled.
And those who hate us,
Have taken plunder for themselves.
¹¹You have delivered us up,
Like animals which are
To be slaughtered for the meat.
And you have scattered us
Among the nations.
¹²You have sold your people off...
For no price at all.
Indeed,
You did not set
Their purchase price high at all.

¹³You have made us
A disgrace to our neighbors
And a source of
Derision and mockery to those
In our neighborhood.
¹⁴You have made us
A proverbial saying
Among the nations,
A cause for the shaking of the head
Among the nations.
¹⁵All day, every day,
My insult...
My disgrace,
Is vividly before me.
And shame covers my face.
In truth,
It has overwhelmed me.
¹⁶From the words of
Those who taunt
And those who revile;
From the presence of
Those who are hostile and
Those who are vindictive.

¹⁷All this has come upon us
And we have not forgotten you.
Nor have we broken faith
With your covenant.
¹⁸Our hearts
Have not turned back,
We have not been disloyal.
Nor have our steps
Turned aside
From your way;
¹⁹That you
Should have crushed us
In the desert,
In the home of jackals.
That you
Should have clothed us
In such an impenetrable gloom,
In the deep and dark shadow
Of extreme danger and death.

[20] If we had forgotten
The name of our God;
If we had ceased to care
And stretched forth
Our hands in prayer
To a god who
Is foreign to us.
[21] Would not God
Have searched this out
And pronounced a judgment?
For he is the one who knows
The secrets of the heart.
[22] But it is for your sake,
On account of our worshiping you,
That we are killed
All day, every day.
And are regarded as animals
For the slaughtering.

²³Be up and moving!
Why will you act as if you sleep?
My Lord,
Wake up!
Do not reject us forever.
²⁴Why will you hide yourself?
Why will you forget
Our misery and our oppression?
²⁵For our soul has sunk
Down into the dust.
Our soulless body
Is struck to the ground.

²⁶Get up!
Be our help!
And redeem us
On account of your faithful graciousness!

# Psalm 45

[1]My heart has been moved
By a good word.
I am reciting my work
Concerning the king.
My tongue is like the pen
Of an experienced and
Skillful scribe.

²You
Have become
More beautiful than
All the sons of men.
Grace and charm
Have poured out
From your lips.
Therefore, our God
Has blessed you forever.

³O valiant one,
Belt your sword into place.
Gird yourself in
Splendor and majesty.
⁴And in your splendor,
Ride on!
Ride forth triumphantly,
On the word of truth
And humble loyalty.
And let your right hand
Point you to
Wonderful and glorious things.

⁵Your arrows are sharpened;
Nations fall under you,
With your arrows in the heart of
The enemies of the king.

⁶Your throne,
Given to you by God,
Is everlasting...
It is for all time.
A scepter of
Fairness and justice
Is the scepter of
Your royal domain.
⁷You love what is right,
You hate what is wrong.
Therefore, our God,
Your God,
Has anointed you
With the oil of
Joy and jubilation.
You have more joy than
Any of your companions.
⁸All your garments
Are fragrant with
myrrh, aloe wood, and cassia.
And, as you come from
Palaces adorned with ivory,
The music of the strings
Causes you to rejoice.
⁹The daughters of kings
Are among your noble attendants.
To your right stands the queen,
Adorned in the finest of gold,
The gold of Ophir.

¹⁰Now listen daughter,
Pay attention and
Listen well.
Forget your people,
Forget your family.
¹¹And the king will greatly desire
Your beauty.

Honor and respect him,
For he is your lord.
¹²And the daughter of Tyre,
The wealthiest of people,
Will come before you
With appropriate gifts.
To both appease you and
Seek your favor.
¹³All will honor you
Princess,
With pearls of coral
And garments of brocade
Laced with gold.

¹⁴She will be brought
Before the king
Clothed in color.
Her virgins,
The attendants who
Accompany her,
Are also being brought
To you.
¹⁵They are brought
In joy and with rejoicing.
They now enter
The palace of the king.

¹⁶You will be revered,
Not for your fathers,
Those who came before;
But for your sons,
Those who come after.
Those whom you trained
And set as princes
Throughout all the earth.

$^{17}$I will praise your name.
Through my work
I will cause it to be remembered
In each and every generation.
Therefore,
The peoples will praise you
Forever and always.

# Psalm 46

¹God is to us
A refuge and protection.
He is a
Strongly proven help
In our times of need.
²Therefore,
We will not fear
When the earth shakes,
When the mountains are shaken
Into the very heart of the sea.
³When its waters chaotically roar
And churn with foam.
Or when the mountains quake
At this roaring.

⁴There is a river;
The canals of which
Cause the city of God,
The holy abode of the Most High,
To rejoice.
⁵It is God
In her midst.
And she will not be shaken.
For God will be her hero
As the darkest of nights
Turns into the bright dawning
Of a new day.

⁶Nations have chaotically roared,
Kingdoms have been shaken.
But at the sound of his voice
The shaking earth melts away
And all is still.
⁷Our Lord,
The Almighty,
Is with us.
The God of Jacob
Is our place of refuge.

⁸Go!
See the work of our Lord!
He has brought to pass
The ruin of the earth shakers.
⁹All over the earth,
He puts away their
Ability to fight.
The bow,
He shatters into many fragments.
The spear,
He smashes to pieces.
As for shields,
He burns them with fire.
¹⁰He says,
"Stop! Be still!
And know, fully comprehend,
That I am God.
I will be revered among the nations.
I will be revered all over the earth."

¹¹Our Lord,
The Almighty,
Is with us.
The God of Jacob
Is our place of refuge.

# Psalm 47

¹Everyone,
Joyously clap your hands!
Raise your voices to God
With the sound of rejoicing.
²For
Our Lord,
The Most High,
Is a cause for
Astonishment and awe.
He is a great king,
The one over all the earth.
³He conquers the nations for us.
And he places them
Under our feet.
⁴For us,
The pride of Jacob
Whom he loves,
He makes the inheritance
Extensive.

⁵Our victorious God
Has ascended to his throne
Amidst the screaming of joy.
Our Lord
Has made his way up to his throne
Amidst the triumphant sound
Of the horns.

⁶Praise God!
Make music to praise him!
Sing praises to our king!
Sing praises!

⁷Sing praises,
For the king of all the earth;
For our God!
Sing in memory
Of what he has done!
⁸Our God
Is the king over the nations.
Our God
Is seated upon his sacred throne.
⁹The nobility of the nations
Has been assembled,
The people
Of the God of Abraham.
For the rulers of the earth
Belong to God.
He is greatly exalted.

# Psalm 48

¹Great is our Lord
And exceedingly worthy
Of being praised
In the city of God,
His sacred mountain.
²Beautiful and towering,
A source of joy
To all the earth,
Is Mount Zion,
Heaven,
The farthest of the north lands.
The city of the great king.

³Our God
Is within her fortifications
And he has revealed himself
To be our refuge and protection.
⁴Witness this,
The kings set a meeting,
Made their alliances,
And came against us
All at once.
⁵They saw our refuge
And so,
Were frozen with fear.
They were horrified
Out of their senses.
They fled in panic.
⁶Then a trembling
Took hold of them.
One of pain and anguish,
Like that of a woman
In the midst of giving birth.
⁷Just like when,
Using the east wind,
You,
Our Lord,
Smashed into fragments
The mighty ships of Tarshish.

⁸Even as we have heard,
So we have seen
In the city of our Lord,
The Almighty.
In the city of our God,
We have seen that God
Will establish it forever.

⁹Sovereign God,
In the midst of your temple
We have pondered
Your faithful graciousness.
¹⁰Sovereign God,
Just like your name,
Even so, your praise
Reaches as far as
The ends of the earth.
Your right hand is full
Of righteousness and well-being.

¹¹Let Mount Zion
Rejoice
In your judgments against our foes.
Let the daughters of Judah
Shout in jubilation,
Because of your decisions in our favor.

¹²Walk around Zion,
Go all the way around,
¹³And count her towers.
Set yourself upon her ramparts;
Pass through her fortifications.
All for the sake
Of announcing to the next generation
¹⁴That this God,
Our God,
Will always lead us.
He will guide us
Forever and ever.

# Psalm 49

¹Let all the people
Hear this!
Let all the inhabitants
Of the world
Heed this!
²Both the common man
And the distinguished one;
All at once, all together,
The wealthy
And the needy.

³My mouth speaks wisdom;
And the meditation of my heart
Is understanding.
⁴I am giving my attention
To a saying of the wise.
I will open up
Its perplexing phrases,
My solved riddle,
With the music of the harp.

⁵Why will I be afraid
In the days of misfortune?
In the days when
The unjust deeds
Of my betrayers
Surround me?
⁶Of those
Who place their trust
In the strength of their wealth.
Who self-confidently boast
In the abundance of their riches.
⁷For
By offering a ransom
They will certainly not
Redeem themselves from death.
For it is beyond their ability
To pay that ransom
To God.

⁸For too precious and costly
Is the ransom for their life,
⁹That they may live forever.
That they will stay alive
Throughout the ages
And so, never see
Their grave.

¹⁰For as it is seen,
The wise, the insolent, and
The brutishly stupid
All die.
One just as much as any other.
And they all leave
Their wealth to others.
¹¹Their graves are their houses,
Forever.
They are their abode
From generation to generation.

Oh, they proclaim ownership
By placing their names
Upon their lands.
¹²But such a man,
With all his precious items,
He does not see.
He does not understand
That he becomes the same as the cattle
That are destroyed.
¹³That this,
Their way
Is for them a source
Of false self-confidence.
To them and
To those who follow after them,
To those who will rejoice over their words.

¹⁴Death will shepherd them.
Yes, like sheep
He will put them into the pen
That is their grave.
And the upright,
In the morning,
Will rule in spite of them.
Even their form
Will disappear in the grave,
Far from their lofty houses.

¹⁵But
God will redeem me
From the power of the grave.
For he will remove me
From its hand.

¹⁶Do not fear
Because a man gains riches;
Because the riches and splendor
Of his house grows great.
¹⁷For when he dies,
He will take with him
Nothing at all.

¹⁸Though, while living,
He congratulates himself.
And though others will
Throw praise at you
When you do well for yourself.
¹⁹He will go,
Even as the generation
Of his fathers.
They will never again
See the light of day.

²⁰Man,
With his precious items....
And he will not see.
He will not understand
That he becomes the same
As the cattle
That are destroyed.

# Psalm 50

¹God,
Our God,
The supreme God,
Our Lord,
Has spoken.
And he has summoned
To the trial, the whole earth;
From the sunrise to the sunset,
From the east to the west.
²From out of Zion,
The completeness and
Perfection of beauty,
Our God shines forth.
³Our God comes
And he is not deaf
Nor will he be silent.
A consuming fire is before him
And round about him a storm rages.
⁴He calls to the heavens above
And to the earth below.
He calls them to be witnesses
For the judging of his people.
⁵He calls,
"Gather to me
My consecrated community.
Those who have made
A covenant with me
Upon a sacrifice."

⁶And the heavens will declare
The justness of the judgments.
For our God himself,
The keeper of covenants,
Is judge.
⁷"Listen to me my people;
I am speaking.
Listen to me
Israel;
I am admonishing you.
I,
God,
Your God.

⁸I'm not rebuking you
For your sacrifices
Or your burnt offerings;
Which are continuously
Before me.
⁹But
I have no need to receive
A sacrificial bull
From your house,
Nor sacrificial male goats
From out of your enclosures.
¹⁰For all the animals
Of the woodlands
And all the thousands of beasts
On the countless hills
Are all mine.
¹¹I know
All the flying creatures of
The mountains
And all small moving things of
Pasture and field.
¹²If I were to be hungry,
I would not mention it to you;
For all the land of the created world
And the fullness there of
Are mine.

¹³Do I eat the flesh
From the sacrificial bulls?
Or, do I drink the blood
From the sacrificial male goats?
¹⁴Sacrifice
Thanksgiving and praise
To God.
And make good on your vows
To the Most High.
¹⁵And then call upon me
In the day of your trouble and need
And I will rescue you;
And you will honor me."
¹⁶But to the wicked God says,
"What right have you
To recite my prescriptions, my laws?
Or to take up my covenant
With only your lips?
¹⁷And you hate
Training and discipline.
And you cast my words
Behind you in disdain.
¹⁸If you see a thief,
You become his friend.
And you keep company
With those who are committing adultery.
¹⁹You have let loose evil with your mouth.
And your tongue harnesses fraud.

²⁰You speak against
And shame
Your brother.
Against your mother's son,
You impute fault.

²¹You have done these things
And, as I have kept silent,
You've compared me to yourselves.
You've imagined that
I
Am exactly like
You.
But now I will rebuke you.
And I will lay out the case
Right before your very eyes.

²²Make sure you understand this,
You who are forgetting God,
Lest I tear you to pieces
And there be none
Who can save you.
²³He who sacrifices
Thanksgiving and praise
Is he who honors me.
And to he who takes
This correct path,
I will cause him to see
The joy found
In the faithful help
Of
Sovereign God."

# Psalm 51

[1]Be gracious to me,
Sovereign God,
According to your
Loyal faithfulness and goodness;
According to your
Great love and mercy,
Wipe away my transgressions.
[2]Thoroughly wash from me
My guiltiness.
Pronounce me clean from my sin.
Purify me.

[3]For I know my transgressions
And I am ever aware of my sin.
As it constantly and vividly presents itself
To my attention.

[4]Against you,
Against you alone,
Have I sinned.
I have performed
This evil
Before your eyes.
On account of this,
You are right and just
When you speak.
And morally pure
In your passing judgment,
In your condemnation.

⁵Behold,
I was guilty
The day I was brought forth.
Indeed,
I was guilty of sin
At the moment
My mother conceived me.
⁶And behold,
You desired honesty
Even while I was in the womb.
And in that place of security
You were making your wisdom
Known to me.

⁷Cleanse me from my sin;
Give me the purity
Symbolized in the hyssop.
And I will be clean.
Wash me;
Cleanse me.
And I will become
Whiter than snow.

⁸Cause me to hear
Joy
And the cries of jubilation.
So that these old bones,
That you have crushed,
May rejoice again.

⁹Avert your face
From my sins
And wipe
My guilt
From your memory.
Sovereign God,
¹⁰Create for me
A pure heart.
And make anew,
In my inner man,
A frame of mind
That is steadfast
And true.

¹¹Do not cast me away
From your presence.
And do not take from me
Your holy and life-giving spirit.
¹²Restore to me
The joy of your deliverance
And sustain me
By giving me
A ready and willing spirit.

¹³I will teach your ways
To those who are disloyal,
To those who are rebelling.
And, by learning from my example,
The sinners will come back
To you.
¹⁴Sovereign God,
Save me from the guilt
Of bloodshed.
For you are the God of my salvation!
My tongue
Will jubilantly proclaim
Your saving justness.
¹⁵My Lord,
Open my lips
And my mouth will
Proclaim your praise.
¹⁶For you do not desire
A sacrifice,
Or I would give it.
Nor will you accept
A whole burnt offering.

¹⁷The sacrifice you desire,
Sovereign God,
Is a spirit of
Brokenness and humility.
A heart that is no longer self-reliant
And that is humble and contrite.
Sovereign God,
This you will not despise;
This is the way that you regard.

¹⁸Because of the pleasure
You have taken in Zion,
Deal well with her.
Rebuild the walls of faith
In Jerusalem.
¹⁹Then you will take pleasure
In sacrifices
Made from the right spirit;
Whole burnt offerings,
The entire sacrifice.
For then,
The bulls may be presented
Upon your alter.

# Psalm 52

¹Why will you
Boast self-confidently
About your evil,
O strong and valiant man?
The faithfulness of God
Continues all day, every day.

²You plan destruction.
Your tongue,
Like a sharpened razor,
Carries out
Deception and treachery.
³You have loved
Evil
More than
Good.
Lies and deceit
More than
Speaking what is right.
⁴You have loved
All words that
Confuse and devour;
You have loved
A tongue of
Trickery and fraud.

⁵God,
For his part,
Will pull you down.
And your ruin will be...
Forever.
He will tear you away
From your home.
And he will uproot you
From the land of the living.
⁶And the innocent and the just
Will understand and honor God.
And they will laugh
Over the ending of this evil.
And they will say,
⁷"Behold, the one
Who will not set
Sovereign God
As his place of refuge.
But who will trust in
His wealth and his prosperity
For his refuge."

⁸But as for me,
Like a luxuriant olive tree
In the house of sovereign God,
I have trusted in
The faithfulness of sovereign God,
Forever and ever.

⁹Before the faithful,
Because of what you have done,
I will praise you forever.
And I do eagerly wait for you.
My hope is in your character,
In your reputation;
For yours is a good name.

# Psalm 53

¹It is the fool,
The irreligious unbeliever,
Who has said in his heart,
"There is no God."
They have perverted themselves
And they are corrupt.
Their deeds are done in a loathsome
And heinous manner.
There is none truly doing good.

²Sovereign God,
From heaven, has looked down
Upon all of mankind.
To see
If there are any
Having insight;
If there are any
Seeking God.

³But as one,
They have all been disloyal;
They have moved away from God.
They are all morally corrupt,
Tainted, and confused.
No.
There is none truly doing good.
There is not even one.

⁴Have not all those,
Who cause sorrow by doing evil,
Learned their bitter lesson?
Those who devour my people,
Who make a meal out of them
The same as they do with bread;
Those
Who do not call upon sovereign God.

⁵Then they quaked
And trembled with dread,
Where danger had not been.
For sovereign God scattered
The bones of those laying siege.

You
Put them to shame.
For you,
Sovereign God,
Rejected them.

⁶Oh, that God's help for Israel
Would come from Zion now.
For when sovereign God
Restores the fortunes of his people,
Jacob will shout in triumph and
Israel will rejoice.

# Psalm 54

[1]Sovereign God,
Through your name,
Your authority,
Save me.
And with your strength
Plead my cause,
Vindicate me.

[2]Sovereign God,
Hear my prayer!
Listen carefully
To the words of my mouth!

[3]For insolent
And presumptuous strangers
Have risen against me.
And formidable adversaries
Seek my life.
Ones that do not
Pay attention
To you.

⁴But take note,
Sovereign God
Is helping me.
My Lord is found
Moving among those
Who support me.

⁵He will repay my enemies
With their own evil.
My Lord,
With your faithfulness
Ruin them.

⁶I will sacrifice to you,
Not from compulsion
But voluntarily...
Of my own free will.
And I will praise your name,
My Lord.
For it is good.

⁷For he has snatched me away
From every enemy.
And my eyes have seen
Their ruin.

# Psalm 55

¹My God,
Heed my prayer.
And do not hide
Your attention
From my pleas for compassion;
²Listen attentively to me
And respond to my plea.

In my lament,
I am restless.
I search for you everywhere
And I am driven to distraction
³By the shouts of the enemy.
For they threaten to drop disaster
Upon me.
And in their anger,
They relish being hostile towards me.

⁴Deep within me,
My heart writhes in anguish.
And the dread of death
Has fallen upon me.
⁵Terror and trembling
Have entered into me.
And this shuddering in horror...
Overwhelms me.

⁶And I say,
"Would that someone
Could give me
Wings like a dove.
I, too, would fly away
And settle down
Where it is safe.
⁷Hear this,
I would go so far away;
To escape all this...
I would spend my nights
In the remotest wilderness.

⁸I would quickly seek out
A place of refuge
From this wind
That is sweeping me away,
From this tempest."

⁹Confuse them,
My Lord.
Divide their thoughts
From their tongues.
For I have seen
Their violent wrongs
And their contentious disputes
In the city.

¹⁰Day and night,
For its protection,
The guards march around
Upon its walls.
But the looming disaster,
The harm, and mischief
Are within its very heart.
¹¹Ruin has engulfed
The heart of the city.
Oppression and fraud
Do not leave the public square.

¹²For it is not an enemy
Who taunts me.
That I could endure.
It is not my enemy
Who has made himself appear great
By doing this great evil against me.
I could hide my heart from him.

¹³But it was you,
A man much like myself,
A close friend
And my confidant.
¹⁴One with whom...
Together
We kept close company,
We had a sweet friendship.
Together
We walked with
The worshiping congregation
To the house of God.

This has vanished
In the tumult.

¹⁵Devastation will come upon them.
While they yet live,
They will go down into
The realm of the dead.
For that which is harmful,
An evil,
Is in their hearts and minds;
It is deep within them.

¹⁶As for me,
I will call on God
And my Lord
Will save me.

¹⁷Throughout the day,
Morning, noon, and in the evening,
I will passionately lament;
And I will murmur softly.
And he will hear my cries;
He will hear my voice.
¹⁸He will rescue my soul
Intact,
From those who are approaching me.
Even though
They have come at me
En masse.

¹⁹For God,
Who abides enthroned
From the most ancient of days,
And with whom there
Is no change,
Will hear and
Bring them down.
For they have
No reverence for
God.

[20] My friend...
He attacked those with whom
He was at peace.
He has profaned his covenant;
He has dishonored friendship.

[21] Smooth as butter
Were the words of his mouth.
But in his heart
There was war.
His words...
Were tender and gentle,
More soothing than
Any ointment.
But they were
Drawn swords
And pointed daggers.

²²Cast that which is given to you
Upon our Lord.
And he will support you;
He will sustain you.
He will not allow the devout
To be
Forever shaken.

²³And you,
My God,
You will bring them down
Into the well of the pit.
For men of
Bloodshed, fraud, and treachery
Will not live out
Half their days.

But as for me,
I will trust in you.

# Psalm 56

¹Be gracious to me
My God;
For men tread upon me.
All day long,
The fighting torments me.
²All day long,
My enemies tread upon me.
For there are many fighting
Against me.
And they hold the high ground.

³In this time,
When I become afraid,
I will trust
In you.

⁴In sovereign God...
I will praise his word.
In sovereign God...
I have trusted.
I will not be afraid.
What can mere flesh
Do to me?

⁵All day long,
Those who pursue me
Take counsel together
Against me.
All their intentions
Are for evil.

⁶They band together,
They conceal themselves,
They set watch over
My very steps.
Because they lie in wait
For my very life.

⁷Away from trouble...
Who of them will escape?
Because,
Sovereign God,
When you are angry
You will cause these people
To fall.

⁸You have
Taken into account my misery.
You...
You have
Stored my tears in your bottle.
Are they not recorded
In your book?

⁹Then,
This I have known,
When I call out to you,
My enemies
Will be turned back.
For sovereign God is with me.

¹⁰In sovereign God...
I will praise his word.
In my Lord...
I will praise his word.
¹¹In sovereign God
I have trusted.
I will not be afraid.
What can
Man
Do to me?

¹²Upon me,
Sovereign God,
Are my vows to you.
I will make good on them
With thank-offerings
To you.

¹³For you have rescued
My soul
From death.
Have you not delivered
My feet
From stumbling?
That I may walk
In the presence of
Sovereign God,
In the light of the living.

# Psalm 57

¹Be gracious to me,
Sovereign God.
Be gracious to me;
For it is in you
That I have taken refuge.
And under the protection
Of your caring wings
I will take refuge;
Until the destruction
Passes by.

²I will call out
To my God,
To the Most High,
To the God.
The one who
Makes appropriate returns
For actions taken
Against me.

³He will send from heaven
And save me from this evil.
He will cause those
Seeking my life
To be disillusioned.
Sovereign God
Will send
His gracious mercy
And his faithfulness.

⁴In the middle of lions
Is where I am.
I must lay down among men
Who are greedy to devour.
Whose teeth are
Spears and arrows.
Whose tongues are
Sword sharp.

⁵Sovereign God,
May you be exalted
Higher than the heavens.
And your glory...
Over all the earth.

⁶They had spread a net
For my feet.
I was sorely depressed.
But
Into the middle
Of the pit,
Which they had dug
Before me,
They have fallen.

⁷My heart is unwavering,
Sovereign God,
My heart is steadfast.
I will sing
And I will sing praises!
⁸All that is honorable within me,
Awaken!
Harp and lyre,
Awaken!
I will awaken
The dawn!

⁹My Lord,
I will praise you
Among the nations.
I will sing praises to you
And not just to your tribes.
¹⁰For your great mercy
Reaches higher than the heavens
And your constant faithfulness,
Higher than the clouds.

¹¹O God,
May you be exalted
Higher than the heavens.
And your glory…
Over all the earth.

# Psalm 58

[1]Really?
When it comes to speaking
About what is right...
Silence?
And you will judge
Your fellow man
Justly?
[2]No.
You practice
Dishonesty and injustice
In your hearts.
Your hands dispense
Violence and wrong
Upon the land.

³From birth,
The wicked
Turned aside
And went astray.
From their birth,
They have wandered off
Speaking lies.

⁴The venom of those lies
Is like the venom of
A snake.
And they have shut up
Their ears and so
Are like
The venomous cobra
Who is deaf.
⁵The one
That will not pay heed
To the sound of
The snake charmers;
That will not be controlled.
Even by one well trained
In snake charming.

⁶Sovereign God,
Break off the fangs
That are in their mouths.
Yes
My Lord,
Smash and make useless
The jaws of these
Aggressive young lions.
⁷Let them err
In their plans.
Let them...
Be like the runoff water
That flows away
And disappears.
Like...
The dried-up grass
On which one treads.
⁸Like...
A harmless snail
That goes about
In its own slime.
They are
The miscarriage of a woman.
They have never truly seen the sun.

⁹Quicker than
They can feel the touch
Of a thorn when
The whole brush seems alive,
Sovereign God,
As with a burning anger,
Will sweep them away
In a whirlwind.

¹⁰The one devoted
To God
Will rejoice.
Because,
He will have seen
The divine retribution.
He will walk
In vindication,
Rejoicing in the
Triumph over
The guilty.

¹¹And men will say,
"Surely, this is
The fruit of and for
Being devoted.
Surely, sovereign God
Is executing
Upright judgment
On the earth."

# Psalm 59

¹My God,
Deliver me
From my enemies.
From those who are
Rising up against me;
Set me high up
And out of reach.
²Deliver me
From those performing
The injustice.
And from
These men of murder,
Save me.

³Take note
My Lord,
They have set an ambush
For my life.
Fierce and strong,
These men
Will attack me.
Not for
My being guilty of a crime
And not for my sin.
⁴I am without guilt.
Yet, they run and
Take up their positions.
Stir yourself
To meet me and see.

⁵ And you,
My Lord,
Sovereign God
Almighty,
God of Israel,
Awaken to this;
To visit and
Call to account
All people of every nation.
Do not show favor to any
Who are dealing treacherously
In wickedness.

⁶And these...
They will return
In the evening.
They will growl and bark
Like dogs;
As they prowl
The city.
⁷Take note.
Through their mouths
Reckless utterances gush forth,
Swords upon their lips.
For who, hearing them,
Will act to stop them?

⁸But you,
My Lord,
Are not bothered by them.
You laugh and
Are at ease.
For you hold these thoughts,
Those of all these people,
In disdain.

⁹The strength of my Lord!
For you
I will keep watch.
For sovereign God,
You are my refuge.
¹⁰The God of my faithfulness
Will come to meet me
And go before me.
Sovereign God
Will cause me to
Look upon my enemies
In joyful triumph.

¹¹Do not
Punish them with death;
Lest my people forget this.
By your power,
Make them unstable in their way;
Cause them to wander about
And cause them to fall.
My Lord,
You are our protection.

¹²Oh,
The sin
Of their mouths,
The words
Of their lips.
Let them be overpowered
And trapped
Through their own arrogance.
Because of the curses and lies
They tell.
¹³In burning anger,
Destroy their abilities.
Bring this evil
To an end;
And they will be…
As if they are no more.
That they may know
To the ends of the earth,
That sovereign God
Is ruling in Jacob.

¹⁴And then,
They will return
In the evening.
They will growl and bark
Like dogs;
As they prowl
The city.
¹⁵They will roam around
Looking for something to eat.
And they will spend the night
Yelping
When they do not
Find enough to satisfy.

¹⁶But, as for me,
I will sing the praises
of your might.
And, in the morning,
I will joyfully proclaim
Your faithfulness.
For you have been
A refuge for me,
A place of safety
In the day of my distress.

¹⁷My strength!
I will praise you
With music!
For, Sovereign God,
You are my refuge,
The God of my faithfulness.

# Psalm 60

[1]Sovereign God,
It is as if
You have disdainfully
Rejected us.
You have violently burst
Upon us in judgment.
As if you have been angry....
Turn back to us,
Bring restoration to us.

[2]You have caused
The land to quake;
You have split it open.
Heal those fissures.
For the land now totters
Back and forth.
It is
Ready to fall.

³You have caused your people
To experience hardship.
You have given us
The wine of staggering
To drink.
Because of this,
We now stagger about
As if we were drunk.
⁴You had given a banner
To those who honor you.
That they might seek
Refuge under it from
The archer's arrows.

⁵In order that
The ones you love
Become delivered,
Respond to us
And save us.
By the power of your right hand.

⁶Sovereign God has spoken
In his holy temple.
"I will lead them.
I will divide up
Shechem.
I will measure up
And parcel out
The valley of Succoth.
⁷For Gilead
Belongs to me.
And Manasseh
Belongs to me.
All of this land
Belongs to me.
And Ephraim
Is the stronghold of
My warriors.
And Judah
Is the house of
My commander.

⁸Of Moab,
It is the basin used
To wash my feet.
Upon Edom
I will cast my sandal,
Upon this, my footstool.
Over Philistia,
Because of me,
You will shout
In triumphant jubilation."

⁹But
Who will bring me
That fortified city?
Who will lead me
To Edom?
¹⁰For sovereign God,
Have you not rejected us?
And sovereign God,
You will not go out
With our troops.

¹¹God,
Give to us
Help against this enemy.
For worthless is the
Help to be found
In any human effort.

¹²With sovereign God,
We will perform bravely.
For it is he
Who will trample down
Our foes.

# Psalm 61

¹Sovereign God,
Hear my impassioned cry,
My lament!
Listen attentively
To my prayer!
²My heart is languishing.
From the extreme end
Of the earth
I cry out to you,
"Help!"
Place me at rest
In that mountain refuge.
The one that is too high
For me to reach alone.

³You have been
A place of refuge for me,
A fortified tower
In the face of the enemy.
⁴Let me,
The foreign guest that I am,
Remain in your tent forever.
Let me
Take refuge in the shelter of
Your wings.

⁵For you,
Sovereign God,
Have listened to my vows.
You have granted the desire
Of those who revere
Your name.
⁶You have added
Extra days to
The days of this king.
And you will add
To his years as well.
Adding, as it were,
A generation and generation
Of years.
⁷Sovereign God,
May he forever
Dwell in your presence.
Send graciousness
And faithfulness
To keep watch over him.

⁸For I will ever
Praise your name
As I fulfill my vows
Day by day.

# Psalm 62

[1]Only for
Sovereign God
Does my soul
Become still and silent.
For only
From him does
My help
And deliverance come.

[2]He alone is
My fortress,
My help and deliverance,
My refuge.
So, I will not be
Exceedingly troubled.

³So,
You will make your
Attacks against a man...
Until when?
You will frequently
Be murderous...
Until when?
All of you,
Every one of you,
Are like a wall
That is bending over;
An old stone wall
That is being pushed in.

⁴Their only plan is
Deception.
They take pleasure in
Seducing with falsehood.
With their mouths
They will praise and bless.
But
From the core of their being,
They declare you
Accursed and contemptible.

⁵Of
Sovereign God
Alone,
Does my soul
Have its silence and rest.
Because
My hope
Is from him,
Alone.
⁶He alone is
My fortress,
My help and deliverance,
My refuge.
I will not
Be troubled.
⁷Sovereign God
Is the reason for
My deliverance
And my honor.
He is the fortress
Of my protection.

My refuge is in
Sovereign God.

⁸My people,
At all times trust in him.
Pour out all that is in your heart
Before him.

For
Sovereign God
Is our refuge.

⁹Mankind
Is nothing but a vapor,
A mere puff of air.
Human beings
Are as dependable as
A lie.
When placed all together,
On one scale,
They are less than
Nothing.

¹⁰Nor trust in
Forcing others
To your will.
And, in gains ill-gotten....
Put no trust in such vanity.
If your wealth does grow,
Do not set your
Heart upon it.

¹¹Sovereign God
Has spoken once
And twice I have heard:
That might
Belongs to God.

¹²And to you,
My Lord,
Belongs mercy and
Faithfulness.
For you,
My Lord,
Give to a man
The reward he is due;
One based upon what he
Has chosen to do.

# Psalm 63

[1]Sovereign God,
My God,
It is for you
That I watch.
It is for you
That my soul thirsts.
My body grows faint
From this longing.
I am in a land of
Drought and exhaustion.
A land where no water is.

²So,
I have seen you
In your holy sanctuary;
Beholding both
Your might and your glory.
³Your gracious faithfulness
Is better than life itself.
My lips will sing
Praises to you.
⁴Thus, will I praise you
In this life;
I will raise my hands
To your name.

⁵I am well satisfied with you.
As if I had eaten
An abundance of
Rich and succulent food.
And with rejoicing lips
My mouth will praise you;
⁶If I but think of you
As I rest upon my bed.
In the dark watches of the night,
I will meditate on you.

⁷Because
You have been
The one who helps me.
And in this protection,
The shadow of your wings,
I continue to cry out
In ringing jubilations.

⁸My soul,
All of who I am,
Holds on to you.
Because
Your right hand
Has taken hold of me.

⁹But they,
Those who seek my ruin,
Will enter into
The depths of the earth.
¹⁰They will be handed over
To the custody of the sword.
Unburied and unhonored,
They will belong
To the jackals.

¹¹But the king
Will rejoice in sovereign God.
All those faithful to him,
All those who swear by him,
Will boast about him.
For the mouths of the liars
Will be stopped.

# Psalm 64

[1]Sovereign God,
Hear the lament in my voice.
Keep watch over my life.
Guard my life
From the dread of
An enemy.
[2]Conceal me
From the secret plotting
Of those doing evil things.
From the unrest and agitation caused
By those
Committing injustice.
By those
Practicing deception.
[3]By those
Who have sharpened
Their tongues
As one would sharpen
The sword.
By those
Who have bent
Their bow in readiness.
Whose arrows are
Bitter words.
[4]Used from concealment
To shoot suddenly,
Surprising the innocent.
To shoot at him
Without being afraid.

⁵They strengthen themselves
With words of little worth.
They talk of
Secretly laying out snares.
They have said, to themselves,
"Who will ever notice them?"
⁶They have
Thought out and examined
What they have hidden.
And say to themselves,
"We have executed
A well-designed plan.
For we are clever;
The depth of our reasoning
Is unfathomable."

⁷But
Sovereign God
Will shoot an arrow at them.
He will shoot suddenly.
And surprising to them
Will be their wounds.
⁸His arrows will cause
Their own tongues,
Those finely honed swords,
To bring ruin upon themselves.

⁹And then, they will be afraid.

And everyone will talk
About God's action here.
And they will understand
What he has done.

¹⁰The devout will rejoice
And take refuge
In our Lord.
And about him,
All of the upright in heart,
Will boast.

# Psalm 65

¹Sovereign God,
To you
Belongs our stillness in waiting.
To you
Belongs our song of praise.
And to you
Our vows will be fulfilled in Zion.
²To you,
The one listening intently
To our prayers.
To you
All people will come.
³For the matter of
Our sinful guilt
Had overwhelmed us.
And now,
You have forgiven
Our transgressions.

⁴Happy and blessed are those
Whom you will choose
And allow to approach.
They will inhabit your courts.
They will have enough,
They will be satisfied
With the best things of
Your house,
Your holy temple.

⁵With terrible and awe-inspiring deeds,
With loyalty,
You answer us.
God of our deliverance,
You are trust;
You are hope,
To the furthest ends of the earth,
Even unto the remotest of seas.
⁶You, who,
Through your own strength,
Created the mountains.
Being clothed in strength,
⁷You calm
The crashing roar of the seas,
The chaotic roar of their waves,
And the chaotic turmoil of the nations.
⁸And those living at
The ends of the earth
Become awestruck;
They tremble
At your miraculous signs.
From where the sun rises
To where it sets,
From east to west,
You cause them
To shout for joy.

⁹You have paid attention
To the earth.
You have caused its abundance;
You have made it exceedingly rich.
The channel of water,
That sovereign God provides,
Is full of water.
Sovereign God,
You have provided the grain.
For you
Have prepared the earth.
¹⁰You thoroughly water
The seeded rows;
Smoothing out the furrows.
You soften the ground
With an abundance of rain.
You bless what grows.
¹¹You have crowned the year
With your goodness.
Along your paths abundance flows.
¹²Abundance also flows
In the pastures of the wilderness.
And the hills
Are enveloped with rejoicing.
¹³The meadows
Are clothed with flocks.
The valleys
Are covered with grain.
They shout for joy.
Indeed, they sing for it.

# Psalm 66

¹All you people
Of the earth,
Shout with rejoicing
To sovereign God.
²Praise
The honor of his name
In song.
Make his praise glorious.
³Say,
To sovereign God,
"How dreadfully awesome
Are your deeds.
Even your enemies,
Though not from loyalty
But because of your great might,
Will pay homage to you.
⁴All the people
Of the earth
Will bow themselves
In worship
Of you.
They will sing
To you.
They will sing praises to
Your name."

⁵Come and see
The deeds of sovereign God!
Dreadful and awe-inspiring
Are his deeds
Among the sons of man.
⁶He changed the sea into dry land.
And through the river
They passed on foot.
There we rejoiced in him;
⁷The one who,
Through his own strength,
Rules forever.
And his eyes are
Examining the nations.
Those who are being stubborn,
Do not exalt yourselves.

⁸People,
Bless our sovereign God!
And cause the voice
Of his praise
To be heard.
⁹Of he who
Sets our souls in life
And who does not permit
Our feet to stumble.

¹⁰For sovereign God,
You have examined us.
You have refined us
Just as silver is refined.
¹¹You led us
Into the net.
You placed afflictions
On our backs.
¹²You caused men to drive
Over our heads.
We went
Through the fire
And through the water.
And you have led us out
Into great abundance.

¹³I will come into your house
With burnt offerings.
I will fulfill my vows to you;
¹⁴That which my lips spoke
And my mouth promised
In my distress.
¹⁵I will present to you
Burnt offerings of fatling sheep
And the
Aromatic smoke of rams.
I will prepare and offer
Oxen and goats.

¹⁶All you,
Who revere sovereign God,
Come and listen!
And I will recount
What he has done for me.
¹⁷To him my mouth called out.
And from my tongue
He was greatly praised.
¹⁸If I had been aware of
Sin in my heart,
My Lord would not
Have listened to me.
¹⁹However,
God has listened.
He has listened attentively
To the voice of
My prayer.

²⁰Praised and adored is
Sovereign God.
Who has not rejected
My prayer.
Who has not removed
His faithful goodness
From me.

# Psalm 67

¹Sovereign God
Will be gracious to us
And he will bless us.
He will make his face
To shine its light
Towards us.

²That your way will be known
Upon the earth.
That your help will be known
Among all the nations.

³Sovereign God,
Let the peoples praise you!
Let all the peoples praise you!
⁴Let the nations rejoice
And shout for joy!
For you will judge
All peoples fairly.
And you will lead
All nations upon the earth.
⁵Sovereign God,
Let the peoples praise you!
Let all the peoples praise you!

⁶The earth
Has yielded its produce.
Sovereign God,
Our God,
Has blessed us.

⁷Sovereign God
Has blessed us.
Let all,
To the ends of the earth,
Tremble in honor of him.

# Psalm 68

¹Sovereign God
Will appear.
And those who are
Hostile to him
Will disperse.
And those
Who hate him
Will flee
From his presence.

²Just like smoke
Is driven away,
You will drive them away.
Just like wax melts away
From before a fire,
The guilty will be carried off
From before the presence of
Sovereign God.

³But the innocent,
The devout,
Will be merry and rejoice
In the presence of God.
They will rejoice
With great mirth and jubilation.

⁴Sing to
God!
Sing praises to
His name!
Prepare the way for
He who drives on the clouds.
His name is
Lord.
Triumphantly rejoice
In his presence!

⁵Father to the fatherless
And protective judge
For the widows.

Sovereign God
Is in his holy dwelling.

⁶Sovereign God
Causes the isolated wanderers
To dwell in a home.
He brings the prisoners out
Into happy prosperity.
But the stubborn,
They inhabit a land
Stripped bare and burned.

⁷Sovereign God,
When you went forth
Before your people,
When you strode
Through the wilderness,
⁸The earth shook;
Yes, and the heavens opened up
Before your presence.
Sovereign God,
The one from Sinai.
Sovereign God,
The God of Israel.
⁹Sovereign God,
You have caused
Rains of abundance to fall.
You have revived
Your wearied people.
¹⁰And we now dwell
In your land of promise.
For in your goodness and kindness
You prepared it for us,
The poor and the needy.

¹¹Our Lord gave the word
And the women, who
Celebrate and herald these glad tidings,
Were great in number.
Shouting,
¹²"The kings and their armies,
They retreat, they flee!"
And at the entrance hall of
The house,
They divided the plunder given.

¹³Even when you were lying
Among the ash heaps,
You were given
The wings of a dove
Overlaid with silver.
And with its pinions
Overlaid with a yellow-green gold.

¹⁴When the Almighty
Scattered the kings in the land,
It was like
How the snow scatters
As it falls on Mount Zalmon.

¹⁵Most beautiful of mountains,
Is the mountain of Bashan.
A mountain range of many peaks,
Is the mountain of Bashan.
¹⁶Why
Do you watch with
Contemptuous envy,
O mighty mountain range,
The mountain God
Has desired to sit upon?
Yes, our Lord
Will sit enthroned there
Forever.

¹⁷The chariots of sovereign God
Are immense in number,
Thousands upon thousands.
Our Lord is with them;
Even as he was at Sinai,
In the holy place.

¹⁸Sovereign God,
You ascended
The heights of the mount
And you have taken them captive.

You have received and given
Gifts among men,
Even among the stubborn.
Your gift to them,
Our Lord,
Sovereign God,
Is to dwell among them.

¹⁹Blessed and praised
Is our Lord.
The God who,
Day by day,
Brings to us our help.
²⁰Our God
Is to us
The God of deliverance.
And to our Lord,
The Lord,
Belong the ways of
Escaping from death.

²¹But
To his enemies,
Sovereign God
Is the way of death.
Their heads he will smash.
Those proud hairy crowns
That walk continuously on
In their offenses,
In their guilty ways.

²²The Lord says,
"From Bashan,
I will bring them back.
From the ocean's depths
I will bring them back.
²³So that your feet will walk
In total triumph,
Walking all over the enemy.
The triumph will be so complete,
Even your dogs will receive
A portion from it."

²⁴Sovereign God,
The people have seen
Your marching procession.
The marching procession of
My God,
My king,
Marching into the holy sanctuary.
²⁵Up in front came
Those who were singing.
Following behind,
Those playing the strings.
And throughout the midst,
The young women,
Those playing the tambourines.

²⁶Praise sovereign God
In the congregation!
Praise our Lord
In the assembly of Israel!
²⁷There is Benjamin,
The least is in the lead.
There are the leaders of Judah,
Their noisy throng!
The leaders of Zebulon
And of Naphtali,
All of Israel is there.

²⁸Your sovereign God
Ordained your strength.

Sovereign God,
You have shown yourself strong
By that which you have done
For us,
²⁹From your temple
In Jerusalem.

To you will the kings bring tribute.

³⁰You have rebuked
Those wild animals of the reeds,
The pack of the mighty,
Along with the young bulls
Of the people.
Having trampled them,
They now bring to you
Pieces of silver.
You have scattered
The people who
Took pleasure in
Engaging us in battle.

³¹Bronze and red cloth
Will come from Egypt.
And Ethiopia will run
To bring the gifts in her hands
To God.

[32] Kingdoms of the earth,
Sing to sovereign God!
Sing praises to Our Lord!
[33] He, who drives in the heavens,
In the heavens most ancient.

Lo,
He raises his voice,
A mighty voice.

[34] Ascribe strength
To sovereign God.
His eminence is over Israel
And his might is in the skies.

[35] Sovereign God,
You are awe-inspiring
From your sanctuary!
The God of Israel,
He is the one bestowing
Strength and power
To his people.
Blessed be
Sovereign God!

# Psalm 69

¹Sovereign God,
Save me!
For the turbulent waters have risen
To the point of threatening
My very soul.

²I have sunk down
Into the mire found
In the depths.
And there is no firm ground
On which to stand.
I have come into
Deep, deep water.
And the flood
Overwhelms me.

³I have grown weary
From calling out to you.
My throat has become hoarse;
My eyes fail me
From watching expectantly
For the arrival of
My God.

⁴Those hating me without cause
Have become more numerous than
The hairs on my head.
Beyond counting,
Is the number of those
Seeking to destroy me.
Those hostile to me...
Are so, wrongfully.
And they do so with lies.
That which I did not steal
I must restore.

⁵Sovereign God,
You have known my foolishness
And my guilt.
For things I've actually done,
Have never been hidden form you.
But these are not what is spoken.

⁶My Lord,
The Lord of Hosts,
The Lord Almighty,
Do not let those
Who are awaiting you
Become ashamed
Because of my mistreatment.
God of Israel,
Do not let those who are seeking you
Become dishonored and confused
Because of my mistreatment.

⁷Because...
It is for your sake
That I have endured disgrace;
That stigma and humiliation
Have covered over my reputation,
Have overwhelmed me.

⁸I have become estranged
From my brethren
And a stranger to
The sons of my mother.

⁹Because of
A passionate zeal for
Your house
Which has consumed me.
And so, the reviling taunts of
Those taunting you
Have descended upon me.

¹⁰When I have wept
And my soul abstained from
All but you.
This was made into
A source for my disgrace.
¹¹When I was clothed in grief,
In grief and repentance,
For my foolishness and
The things I've actually done.
Then I became to them
A proverb,
A notorious example,
A byword,
By their lies.
¹²It has become the business of the day
For those sitting in the city gate
To speak mockingly of me.
And for those drinking too much
To do so in song.

<sup>13</sup>But as for me,
My prayer to you,
My Lord,
Is for a time of your good favor.
Sovereign God,
In the great abundance of
Your faithful goodness,
Answer me
With the faithfulness of your help.
<sup>14</sup>Rescue me from the mire
That I may not sink down.
That I may be delivered
From those how hate me
And from these
Deep, deep waters.

<sup>15</sup>Do not let these flood waters
Overwhelm me.
And do not let this depth
Engulf me.
And do not let this watery pit
Close its mouth over me.

<sup>16</sup> Answer me,
My Lord!
According to the greatness of
Your compassionate mercies,
Turn your attention
Towards me.
<sup>17</sup> And do not hide yourself
From me, your servant.
For distress is upon me.
Make haste!
Answer me!
<sup>18</sup> Draw close to me!
Redeem my life!
With reference to my enemies,
Ransom me!

[19] For you know
My disgrace, my shame,
And the reproach I bear.
And you know
All of my adversaries.
[20] Disgrace has broken my heart
And now, I am in despair.
I eagerly looked for sympathy
And there was none.
I eagerly looked for those
Who would give comfort
And I found none.
[21] Instead,
They gave me,
As a meal given by
Sympathetic friends,
Bitter and poisonous herbs.
And to quench my thirst,
They gave me vinegar to drink.

<sup>22</sup>Let their own worship table
　Become a trap unto them.
And let their peace offerings
　Become their own snare.
<sup>23</sup>Let their eyes
　Grow dim from searching.
Cause their strength to be
　Continuously shaken.
<sup>24</sup>Cause your indignation
　To flow upon them
And your burning anger
　To collect them.
<sup>25</sup>May their fortified camp
　Be made desolate.
And in their tents,
　May none dwell.

<sup>26</sup>For the one whom you
　Have smitten and corrected,
They have maliciously pursued.
　And to the pain
Of the one you have pierced,
　They only add yet more pain.
<sup>27</sup>Grant to them punishment,
　Upon what is punishable.
And do not let them enter
　Into your leniency.
<sup>28</sup>Let them be wiped out
　From the book of those who live.
And in the company of the devout,
　Do not let them be recorded.

²⁹But as for me,
Though I am afflicted
And though I am in pain,
You,
Sovereign God,
Will help me.
You will make me inaccessible.
You will set me securely on high.
You will protect me.

³⁰I will praise the name
Of sovereign God
In song.
And I will
Honor and praise him
With a song of thanksgiving.
³¹And this will be
More pleasing to you,
My Lord,
Than any sacrifice
Of an ox or young bull;
One with horns fully grown
And hoofs that are cloven.

³²The dejected will see this
And they will rejoice.
And to those seeking to worship
Sovereign God,
Let your hearts
Be strengthened and
Beat strong.
³³For my Lord
Directs his hearing
Towards the needy.
And he
Does not despise his own;
Those who are prisoners of
Affliction and need.

³⁴Let heavens, earth, and seas,
And everything that moves therein
Praise him.
³⁵For sovereign God
Will deliver Zion
And will rebuild
The cities of Judah.
And they, his people,
Will dwell there
And will possess it.
³⁶And the children of
His servants will inherit it.
And those loving his name
Will dwell in it.

# Psalm 70

¹Sovereign God,
To rescue me...
My Lord,
To my aid
Make haste.

²Let those seeking
My life
Be put to shame
And disgraced.
Let those desiring
My misery and misfortune
Be turned back,
Driven backwards,
And humiliated.
³Let those maliciously saying,
"Aha, aha!"
Be turned back.
On account of...
As the wages of
Their shame.

⁴Let those who are
Searching for you
Rejoice
And rejoice
Because of you.
And let those who love
Your help
Continually say,
"Sovereign God is great."

⁵But as for me.
I am afflicted
And in need of help.
Sovereign God,
Hurry to me.
My help,
And my deliverer,
You,
My Lord,
Do not delay.

# Psalm 71

¹In you,
My Lord,
I have taken refuge.
For that,
Never let me be put to shame.
²With your saving justness,
Pull me out of this
And deliver me.
Bend your ear to me
And save me.
³Be to me...
As a fortified dwelling
To continuously come to;
The one you have appointed
For my deliverance.
For you are
My protective cliff
And you are
My mountain stronghold.

⁴My God,
Deliver me
From the hand of
The wicked,
From the power of
Those acting
Unjustly and oppressively.
⁵For you are
My hope
O Lord,
My Lord,
The object of my confidence,
From my youth.

⁶From my birth
I have braced myself
Upon you.
From my mother's womb
You pulled me out, cut me loose.
My songs of praise
Are continuously
About you.

⁷I have been
A sign and a wonder
To many.
Since you are
My fortified refuge.

⁸My mouth is filled with
Praise of you.
All day long
It is filled with
Your honor and glory.

⁹Do not cast me off
In this time of old age.
Do not leave me behind
As my strength and abilities
Fade.

¹⁰For my enemies
Have spoken against me.
And those seeking my life
Have taken counsel together
¹¹Saying,
"God has left him behind.
Pursue and seize him!
For there is none now
To save him."
¹²Sovereign God,
Do not be distant from me.
My God,
Hurry to my aid.
¹³Let them be ashamed.
Let them fade;
Those who are
The adversaries of my soul.
Let those seeking my misfortune
Cover themselves with
Shame and disgrace.

¹⁴But, as for me,
I will continually wait
For you.
And I will add to all of
Your songs of praise.
¹⁵My mouth will proclaim
Your loyal justness.
All day long,
It will make known
Your help and deliverance.
Even though I do not know
How to write in a manner
Which can fully
Praise them.

¹⁶I will come.
Because of the
Miraculous deeds of
The Lord,
My Lord.

¹⁷Sovereign God,
You have taught me
From my youth.
And even now,
I still proclaim
Your miraculous deeds.

¹⁸ And even now, as I am aging,
Becoming old and grey,
Sovereign God,
Do not leave me behind
While I declare your strength
To a future generation;
While I praise your might
To all who are to come.

¹⁹ And your justness,
Sovereign God,
Reaches up to
The heights of heaven.
As to the great things
Which you have done,
Sovereign God,
Who is like you?

²⁰You,
Who has caused me
To experience afflictions,
Both ample and sinister.
You
Will reverse these actions, again.
And will restore life to me.
You
Will return to me, again.
And will pull me up from
The abyss of the earth.
²¹You will increase my greatness.
That is,
You
Will turn again, towards me.
You
Will comfort me.

²²Therefore,
I will praise you,
With the instrument of music,
With the harp.
For your faithfulness,
My God,
I will play songs about you
With the lyre.

Holy one of Israel,
²³My lips will sound
A ringing cry of
Joyous exultation!
Yes,
I will sing to you,
With my lips and my life.
Which,
You
Have redeemed.
²⁴Also, all the day long,
My tongue will proclaim
Your loyal justness.
For they have been put to shame.
Indeed,
They have been shamed;
Those who have been striving
To bring me harm.

# Psalm 72

¹Sovereign God,
Give to the king
Your judgments
And your justness
To this royal son.
²Then he will administer
The help of judgment
To your people,
Through your just loyalty.
And he will help
Your poor and needy
With the judgments.

³Then
The mountains and the hills
Will yield peace and deliverance
To the people,
Through justice.

⁴Then
He will provide
The poor and needy of the people
With justice.
He will come
With assistance
On behalf of
The children of the needy.
And he will crush those
Exploiting them.
⁵They will stand
In awe before you;
As long as the sun shines
And the moon rises,
Generation after generation.

⁶Then
He will descend
Like refreshing rain
Upon mown grass.
Like plentiful showers
Watering the land.

⁷Then
In his days,
Just conduct
And well being
Will flourish.
As will an abundance of
Peace and prosperity.
Until the moon ceases to be.

⁸Then
He will rule
From sea to sea.
And from The River
As far as
The very ends
Of the earth.

⁹And
In his presence,
Those who dwell
In the wilderness
Will kneel
In reverence.
And his enemies
Will prostrate themselves
In great humiliation.
Looking like
They're licking the dust.

¹⁰The kings of Tarshish
And of the distant
Coasts and islands
Will give homage,
Will pay tribute.
The kings of
Sheba and Seba
Will bring gifts.

¹¹And before him,
All kings
Will bow low.
All peoples
Will serve him.

¹²Then
He will deliver
Those in need
When they cry out for help;
And the poor
And those with no one
To help them.

¹³For
He will look compassionately
Upon the poor
And upon the needy.
And he will deliver
The lives of those in need.
¹⁴From oppression and violence
He will redeem their lives.
For
In his eyes,
Their life's blood
Is precious.

¹⁵Then
He will live.
And to him gifts will be given
From the gold of Sheba.
And prayers will be
Continuously offered
On his behalf.
And blessing will be
Invoked, all the day long,
Upon him.

¹⁶Then
In the land, there will be
An abundance of grain.
On the mountain tops
It will rustle and wave.
Its fruit will be
As plentiful as that of Lebanon.
And those from the cities
Will flourish.
Just like this abundant growth
From the land.

¹⁷Then
His name will be remembered,
Forever.
His name will be propagated,
It will produce descendants,
As long as the sun shines.
And all peoples
Will bless themselves through him.
And all nations
Will call him blessed.

¹⁸Blessed, praised,
And adored
Is our Lord,
Sovereign God,
The God of Israel.
The one
Who makes
The things of wonder
By himself,
With the help of no one.

¹⁹And blessed
Is the name of
His abundant glory.
And his glory fills up...
The entire world.
Amen and amen!
This is certain,
This is so!

[20] Here ends
The prayers of David,
The son of Jesse.

# References List:

This is the list of the lexicons, the analytical key, commentaries, and some of the Bible translations I used in putting together this presentation. These were used for definitions and to make sure my interpretation of a verse was in keeping with what the text was actually saying. For instance, if I found what I thought a verse to be saying was not supported by any commentaries or the accepted scholarly translations, I jettisoned my thoughts and researched why I got it wrong. Then I studied how the others may have arrived at their understandings. Then, when I understood this, I had an understanding that was in line with established thought. These have proven invaluable for keeping me from going astray; from either adding to or taking away the meanings contained in the Psalms.

## Lexicons

Brown, Francis, S. Driver, and C. Briggs. The Brown-Driver-Briggs. *Hebrew and English Lexicon*. 1906. Reprint, Peabody, MA: Hendrickson Publishers, 2015.

Davidson, Benjamin. *The Analytical Hebrew and Chaldee Lexicon*. Grand Rapids, MI: Zondervan Publishing House, 1979.

Holladay, William L. ed. *A Concise Hebrew and Aramaic Lexicon of the Old Testament*. Leiden, The Netherlands: E.J. Brill, 1988.

Koehler, Ludwig, and Walter Baumgartner. *The Hebrew and Aramaic Lexicon of the Old Testament*. Study ed. Vols. 1 and 2. Edited and translated by M.E.J. Richardson. Leiden, The Netherlands: Koninklijke Brill NV, 2001.

Owens, John Joseph. *Analytical Key to the Old Testament.* Vol. 3, Ezra – Song of Solomon. Grand Rapids, MI: Baker Book House, 1991.

Strong, James. *The New Strong's Expanded Exhaustive Concordance of the Bible.* Nashville, TN: Thomas Nelson Publishers, 2010.

## Commentaries

Barnes, Albert. *Notes on the Old Testament Explanatory and Practical, Psalms.* Vols. 1 and 2. Edited by Robert Frew. 1950. Reprint, Grand Rapids, MI: Baker Book House, 1971.

Kinder, Derek. *Psalms 1-72.* 1973. Reprint, Downers Grove, IL: InterVarsity Press, 2008.

Longman, Tremper III. *How to Read the Psalms.* Downers Grove, IL: InterVarsity Press, 1988.

Longman, Tremper III. *Tyndale Old Testament Commentaries.* Vols. 15 and 16, *Psalms an Introduction and Commentary.* Edited by David G Firth. Downers Grove, IL: InterVarsity Press, 2014.

Longman, Tremper III., and David E. Garland, eds. *The Expositor's Bible Commentary.* Vol 5, *Psalms.* Rev. ed. Grand Rapids, MI: Zondervan, 2008.

Schaefer, Konrad. *Berit Olam Studies in Hebrew Narrative and Poetry, Psalms.* Edited by David W. Cotter. Collegeville, MN: The Liturgical Press, 2001.

Spurgeon, C. H. *The Treasury of David.* Vols. 1 and 2. Peabody, MA: Hendrickson Publishers Marketing, LLC, 2014.

Wilson, Gerald H. *The NIV Application Commentary: Psalms.* Vol. 1. Grand Rapids, MI: Zondervan, 2002.

# Other Resources

Bullinger, E. W. *Figures of Speech Used in the Bible*. Mansfield Centre, CT: Martino Publishing, 2011.

Ryken, Leland, James C. Wilhoit, and Tremper Longman III, eds. *Dictionary of Biblical Imagery*. Downers Grove, IL: InterVarsity Press, 1998.

# Bible Resources

Below is a list of some of the Bible translations that I always keep open as I am reading the Psalms in the Hebrew. If all I had to use were these, I would have been a richly rewarded man. Simply reading several different translations of any given chapter in the Bible provides great insights into what is being said. Insights and nuances missed if all you read is the one translation. Not that only reading one is a bad thing. It too will be richly rewarding to the person who is seeking a relationship with God. But the more of them you read, the more your appreciation, for what is said, can grow. After this list, I'll share two websites that offer free access to all of these and more. As of this writing, here is an alphabetical listing of the translations I currently have open and am using:

1599 Geneva Bible.
Complete Jewish Bible,
Darby Translation,
Holman Christian Standard Bible,
JPS Tanakh 1917,
Lexham English Bible,
New American Standard Bible,
New English Translation,

New Heart English Bible,
New International Version,
New Living Translation,
World English Bible.

I have used others and will use more. But these make for an excellent nuanced understanding of any chapter and verse. And now for the two promised websites.

They are (and these are in no particular order, except alphabetical):

BibleGateway:   https://www.biblegateway.com/

Bible Hub:   https://biblehub.com/


Please note: these websites are third party websites. Charles Yerkes and Simple Not Shallow are not affiliated with nor responsible for any content or links found on them. They are provided for your information only.

www.ingramcontent.com/pod-product-compliance
Lightning Source LLC
Chambersburg PA
CBHW070419010526
44118CB00014B/1818